A Woman's Remarkable Journey to Self- Discovery

Arise

Woman of Worth

Twila R. Favors

Published in the United States by ARISE WOMEN OF
WORTH MINISTRIES LLC
Arise Woman of Worth

Dedications

I dedicate this book to the late Dorothy J. Favors. Mama, you are and forever will be my first love. Our bond began as your blood became my blood. Your nutrients became my nutrients. Your oxygen kept me alive within the womb.

It is my memories of you Mama, that help me to breathe on my own now. Thank you for loving me enough to bring me in this world and to love me so unselfishly every single day of my life.

You showed me how to stand, and how to walk forward, both in the natural and in the spirit.

You poured into me, even when your well was running dry. For this Mama, I thank you with everything within me.

Your class, sass, with just a smidgen of brass, pours forth as every streaming water that gives life, to me, your grandsons, and your new great granddaughter. Mama, you represent everything I have lived for. She represents everything I shall live for.

History meets destiny, and God has blessed me to be the mouthpiece.

Our stories must be told.

Your faith, style, beauty, grace, elegance, perseverance, unconditional love, and unimaginable strength has left a legacy that will never end.

Until we meet again,

rest on my Queen.

Rest On.

Mama, you were my first Woman of Worth.

I love you forever.

-Twi Twi

THANK YOU

"always giving thanks to God the Father for all things, in the name of our Lord Jesus Christ." – Ephesians 5:20 AMP

God, I just want to thank You for loving me for who I am. You love me not only in spite of me, but because of me. You love me because you created me just the way You wanted me to be, flaws and all.

Your love for me remains the same, whether my day is good or bad, and for this I give You praise Lord. Thank You God, for saving my life over and over again.

You are the constant, dependable love of my life. God, I am Yours and You are mine. Nothing can separate the Two of us, and for this I give You praise.

God, I am humbled, honored, and forever grateful, that you have chosen me, a cracked vessel, to shine Your Marvelous Light through in this literary work.

Please be glorified. I thank You for using my Words as a healing balm to the wounded hearts, and inspiring them to Arise and live.

Thank You Lord.

Lela, there are simply no words to describe how much you mean to me. You were the one to push me out in ministry. You were the one that had my back during the seasons that will come out in later books. I shall never forget. I love you forever.

A special thank you to Bishop Robert Lyons, for teaching me sound doctrine through your powerful preaching and teaching of the Word of God. Thank you for being my Spiritual Covering. I love and appreciate you.

To Minister Le Anna White, thank you for being there for me through my wilderness experiences. You spoke life to me when I wanted to die. You were there to feed me when I could not eat, guide me when I could not see, and comfort me when the tears would not cease. I am forever grateful to you for this. I love you.

To my special friends, Deacon Peter Ramos and Elder Debra Ramos, there are no words to adequately describe how much the two of you mean to me. Peter, thank you for offering me so many pep talks, before church on Sundays, during my writing season. I love you both so much.

I want to give a huge thank you to Minister Catherine Storing, my writing coach. Writing Mama, what can I say? Not only did God bless me with a writing coach, he added a loving, bossy, and hilarious sister to my life. You have inspired me more than words can say, to give birth to this baby, without such an incredible *Book Midwife.* Thank you for holding me up when I was too weary to push.

Thank you for not giving up on me, and not allowing me to punk out in this process. You know I was giving you all kinds of eye rolls, and neck turns in the beginning, right? I love that "brown girl attitude!" You were giving me, me!

I want to give a special shout out to my entire Write Your Book in Forty Days Family. Oh My Goodness, Writing Superstars, you all are my Peeps! I am so proud of each one of you for your perseverance, faith, transparency, and accomplishments.

We are family for life. I love you all so much.

Thank you to my Accountability Partner, Deacon Sckeitha Jones. Sis, you have become such a sister-friend in my life. I could not have made this journey without the worship, songs, prayers, and so many words of encouragement.

Thanks for sharing your life with me. Thank you for becoming a true sister and friend to me. You were not about to let me give up in this process. I saw that Facebook Call button more during this forty days, than I have in my *entire* life (smile.) I needed *every* one of those calls.

To my other Accountability Partner, Minister Shirley Williams, listen firecracker, you showed me the God that gives prevailing strength! You are preaching, pressing, and pursuing somebody!

Continue to have undeniable faith in Him, and there is literally nothing you cannot have or do through Him. Girl, your sense of humor, ability to slay a demon, and then, continue a conversation in a matter of minutes, will *never* be forgotten. I love you for life!

Elder Cora Jakes Coleman, thank you for giving me the courage to go about my life, "Faithing It." You were my first mentor! After being hurt and betrayed by a woman in the church, you were the first woman I dared to trust again.

I appreciate you Elder Cora, for speaking to the Woman of Worth within me. Thank you for encouraging me to walk boldly in the gifts that God has placed inside of me.

Elder Cora, thank you so much for forcing me to use my voice. Without you forcing me to press that red Periscope button, I do not know if I would have found the strength to tell my story.

You breathed a spirit of excellency in me that states, "Even if you have to do it afraid, just do it." Thank you. I love you, fierce and anointed Woman of God.

Dr. Gaylena White, you spoke life to the minister in me, who lost her voice. I remember crying to you many times about losing my voice. Your strength, power, and Holy Ghost anointing, defibrillated my quivering heart back to life, on more than one occasion. From the depths of my being, I say thank you. I love you so much. You are a powerhouse for the Kingdom of God!

Coach Misty Goodwin, Prophetess, thank you so much for giving me drink in my dry and parched seasons. God used you to love me, and speak confidence in me. I love you woman of God! Thank you so much!

Pastor Kimberly Jones, OMG! Sis, *And You Shall Decree a Thing,* is the Devotional that gives me life. Without reading the Word of God through your Devotional and decreeing it over my life, I do not know how I would have made it through the *many* attacks on my life and peace of mind during the journey.

Thank you for being obedient to God. Your boldness, helps me to get back to who God created me to be. I love you.

Minister Tina Moore Brown, Thank you for your boldness, transparency, and consistency. You have helped me more than you know.

A special thank you to Jacci Foster-Jackson, for bringing my vision for the book cover to life. You are amazingly gifted. I am so grateful to God for you. Thank you for hanging in there with me, with ALL my book title changes. I love you so much!

To my editor, website designer, and branding expert, thank you so much for helping to get started with my first book! Dawn you are so gifted and talented beyond words. Thank you for being patient with me and answering my *billions* of questions.

Thank you to my oldest son, DeAndre'. Favors for doing this amazing photography for my book cover. Your photography skills are lit! Thank you for allowing the Holy Spirit to direct the Photoshoot that Day.

Your Future is so Amazing in Photography and Videography. I love you tremendously!

Thank You!

Hit DeAndre' up on Facebook or Instagram, you all-Dre' Shot This. I love you Son! Thanks for being proud of me for chasing my dreams! I am equally as proud of you for chasing yours! I love you for life!

Yes, I did a shameless plug (smile.)-Ma Dukes

To my granddaughter Kayla, thank you for helping your Daddy at the Photoshoot and for making me smile!

Also Kayla, thank you for helping your MiMi live again. You made my heart beat stronger. Everyone who is alive, knows you are my girl! I am determined to make sure you *know your worth.* I love you Baby Girl!

A ginormous thank you to my Pastor-Son Devin Favors, who was my biggest cheerleader! Devin, your enthusiasm about my writing, pushed me to the finish line. Mama had to push through! I couldn't let you down. Thank you for believing in me. Thank you so much for praying for me, giving me so many pep talks, and words of encouragement.

Thank you for keeping me on track. You are gifted, far greater than you can see. I love you to life!

To My Baby Son, Darien Favors, thank you for always knowing when I needed that "I love ya" text. Somehow, you always knew when I needed to hear this. I love you too son. I love you to infinity and beyond.

Thank you, Bryttani Sewell, who was also one of my biggest cheerleaders. Daughter, what can I say? I love you beyond words. You have encouraged me so much. I appreciate your many text messages telling me, "You got this!"

No matter what you were going through, you took the time to cheer me on. Brytt, I will never forget this. That is just one of the reasons why you are my Girl for life Boo!!!

LaTeasa R. Spears, my goodness! Hun, I will try not to write a book here. Thank you for being such a sister-friend to me! Thanks for showing me how to become an author! God was definitely up to something, when he introduced us eleven years ago! I appreciate you for encouraging me and answering my millions of questions. I am so proud of you for writing your first book, *Taking the Kingdom by Storm One Godly Marriage at a Time!* I love you to life Girlie!!!

To Erin Williams, thank you for always believing in me daughter! You, beautiful lady, inspired me so much by saying these words, "Mama let me know when you have your book signing. I will be there."

I had not even considered myself a worthy enough author for a *Book Signing*. Erin, you expanded my vision.

It is because of you, Pretty Lady, that I will be having a Book Signing Event. Thank you for helping me work on being an Author of Worth. I'll see you at my Book Release Party girl! (Smile)

I love you and my babies so much. I am so grateful God has brought you all into our lives, Woman of Worth.

To My "Secret" Facebook Group-Thank you so much Ladies, for the encouragement and feedback. I love you ladies forever! Thanks for never giving up on me. Thank you for giving input when I asked for feedback. You ladies rock! With God, I finally finished! Woot Woot!

Dr. Jack Henderson, Sir what can I say? Your generosity touched my heart more than I can say. I tear up every time I tell someone how you invested in me, in such a special way, before I could even explain my vision clearly. Thank you also, for your many words of encouragement, wisdom, and prophecy.

May God open the windows of Heaven and pour out His blessings on you- pressed down, shaken together, and running over!

To My friend Mr. Garry Artis, thank you for always being there for me and my crew. I love you to life. You are a mighty man of God. You encourage me to be a better person, real talk.

Thank you to my Sister-Friend Rhea Monee Atkins! You are the first "real life" Self-Publishing Author I have ever known. I took note, Sis. You are a modern day Virtuous Woman. Thank you for leading me, believing me, and showing me how Bosses get things accomplished. You rock! I love you Queen.

To My God-Daughter Zontaye Richardson, you are another example of a Virtuous Women. You considered a field and bought it. Your younger sisters are showing the clear throat, more "mature" sisters, how to get it done.

Thank you for blessing me to use your boutique for my Book Signing Party. There could not have been a more perfect Venue. I knew I would be surrounded by love and family, while near you.

Your love made my day even more special. Thank you.

Theze Dealz- A Thrifty Boutique was the perfect place to introduce my Baby to the world. Thanks so much for your generosity. I have loved you from Day one...literally (smile.)

I thank God, for the Manifold Blessings He is about to send in your life. You will not have to work, nor sweat for these blessings. They will pour forth like rain on your life. You are a Godsend!

To my Best Friends Deon and Sherry Hunter, thank you for being there for me through it all.

Sherry, we go *way* back. We held each other's newborns, ran the streets, ran from our callings, now we are running to play with our grandchildren. Girl, won't God do it?

It is not often you find true ride or dies. Thank you for being mine.

Thanks for always supporting me in my endeavors. I am not about to write a book about us on this Thank You Page (laughing.) You already know.

Thank you Deon, for loving me and being there through it all. You are my friend. Thanks for the photography at my Book Release Party! - Deon T. Hunter of D&S Photography

Deon and Sherry, may God continue to pour out blessings for you and your family. I love you all for life.

A special thank you to Victoria Hoke and Kimberly Lott for loving me unconditionally, and speaking to the Woman of Worth, I could not see within.

Know that you Queens are more precious than rubies to me. I love you more than words could say. Okay, Care Bear moment over. (Smile)

Last but certainly not least, I must scream Thank You and give a group hug to my Facebook Family! I have bared my soul to you all, and you all did not run away from me. You loved and accepted me, good, bad, and ugly.

You all believed in me, encouraged me, listened to me vent, and told me I could do it. The way you all congratulated me when I announced my Book Release Party, made my heart smile!

I will cherish your love for me, Facebook Family, for the rest of my Days! Chase your Dreams and don't stop until you catch them.

For Everyone,

"Beloved, I pray that you may prosper in all things and be in health, just as your soul prospers." John 3:2

Heavenly Father, you are a great and mighty God. Be glorified in this work. If there is anything displeasing to you, pluck it out before it is ever published. Pour me out as a drink offering to Your people.

I am available to You, oh God. Use me as You will.

Please speak through me, Holy Spirit. Hear the cries of Your people God. We have been crying for too long without hope.

Restore our hope in You. Make us whole. Redirect our thoughts and seal the wounds of our pasts, so they stop oozing sadness, bitterness, and regret.

In the name of Jesus, I pray,

Amen

Preface

I lost my footing. I am not only talking about events that happened to me a long time ago, but also things that occurred not so long ago.

It seems I was always the black sheep. The one that does not quite make the cut. My gifts are not quite what the pastor is looking for. My beauty is not quite what the man is searching for.

My friendship was not good enough. My advice, not wise enough. My love, not deep enough. My singing voice, not strong enough. My body was never good enough. My anointing was not wanted in the church, "there was not room enough" for it.

How am I supposed to know I have worth, when so many discard me like I am trash? I started to believe their views of me.

God said, *"Trust my view."*

My God, where do I fit in? Why did you create me to be the way that I am? Who am I good enough for?

Although, I expected an eloquent response, from so great and magnificent a God. The one that I received, was simple, yet it comforted my very soul. God simply replied, "Me."

Introduction

It is my prayer that as you read my story, I will reveal my authentic heart to you. This, not to draw you to me, but to draw you to God.

It is like, when you go to the doctor's office. The doctor says to the patient, "Show me where it hurts." I do not know about you all, but I have been in some situations when the pain has been too much for me to bear.

I did not know whether it was protocol or not, but I started stripping before the doctor, before he could get a nurse in the room. I was like, "Look, you have got to help me. I cannot deal with this pain." I put all my confidence in the man who was practicing medicine.

How much more do you think the Great Physician will heal us, if we give Him the same confidence and willingness to strip before Him?

God wants us to take self-inventory. Where are we dysfunctional? Where do we keep getting stuck? What mindsets tend to trip us up time, and time again?

We must be willing to get naked before God. We just might as well. He sees all of us anyway. I had gotten myself in so many messes, that I finally volunteered for the strip down.

It was in my willingness to stop hiding from the truth of needing a Divine touch from God, that I found His Hand reaching out to me, calling me to ARISE.

The next hundreds of pages will be a JOURNEY. We will laugh, cry, pray, maybe even want to use some "choice" words. We will walk the tightrope of hope and despair. We will jump in the boxing ring and contemplate whether to sit back in defeat, or glove up for one more round. Queens, this is real life.

I don't mind showing you my scars, it is simply a reminder of my healing. What tried to take me out the game, wasn't strong enough.

Clearly your assassinators, attackers, and accusers weren't strong enough to take you out either because you are reading my book. Arise Woman of Worth. It will get better from here. Your future is much brighter than your past.

But first you must arise.

Then He took the child by the hand, and said to her, "Talitha, cumi," which is translated, "Little girl, I say to you, arise."-Mark 5:41

Chapter One -God Loves *US*

"Who shall separate us from the love of Christ? Shall tribulation, or distress, or persecution, or famine, or nakedness, or peril, or sword? As it is written:

"For Your sake we are killed all day long;

We are accounted as sheep for the slaughter."

Yet in all these things we are more than conquerors through Him who loved us. [38] For I am persuaded that neither death nor life, nor angels nor principalities nor powers, nor things present nor things to come, nor height nor depth, nor any other created thing, shall be able to separate us from the love of God which is in Christ Jesus our Lord." Romans 8:35-39

Growing up insecure, made it difficult to comprehend how such a big God could love such a little old me. But, He did. I cannot pinpoint the exact moment I became unsure of myself. I just know I had issues. Oh, how I wish I knew then, the love of God that I know now. My life would have been so very different.

I have had a difficult time grasping the height, width, and depth of God's love for me. I have read many verses that declare His love. I have worshipped Him and adored Him. I have even preached about the love of God and the fact that God IS love.

Yet, it was hard to apply His unfailing love to *me.* I could see wholeheartedly, why the perfect, forgiving, merciful, beautiful, caring, gracious, Savior would still accept you and see you as His own, but not *me.*

It breaks my heart to type this out. However, this is just how deeply the seed of rejection, self-hatred, and low-self -worth was deposited into me.

Am I the only one?

There is good news today. God loves *us* too. The ones that hide our fragile insecurities, diminished self-confidences, and non-existent identifications as royalty. There is healing for us. God loves us.

He will redeem the time for us. It does not matter how much time we have spent not loving ourselves, He will love us so powerfully, from now forward, the past won't even matter. Queens and Kings, straighten your crowns. We are royalty.

"But you are A CHOSEN RACE, A royal PRIESTHOOD, A HOLY NATION, A PEOPLE FOR God's OWN POSSESSION, so

that you may proclaim the excellencies of Him who has called you out of darkness into His marvelous light;" 1 Peter 2:9 NASB

God's love for us is unfailing. There is nothing we have done that has made Him stop loving us. This is difficult for us to grasp because we compare the agape love of God for us, to the conditional love of man for us.

God's love is unconditional, whole and complete.

It is bigger, wider, and deeper than the mind can comprehend. He cares for us, and wants us to have a blessed and happy life.

God smiles when we smile. He desires for us to know who we are in Him, and to be whole. It grieves the Spirit of God, to see us walking with our Heads bowed down in defeat and despair.

He wonders, "Do they know how much I love them? Why won't they just turn to me for help?"

God desires to help you. Will you let Him?

"God is our refuge and strength [mighty and impenetrable],

A very present and well-proved help in trouble." -Psalms 46:1 AMP

If you have turned away from God, I am begging you, in this season, please turn your hearts back to God. He loves you. God is love. You will never learn to love yourself without first loving God.

It is impossible to love another human being healthily, without first loving yourself. God is needed for the love equation.

We are valuable in the heart, mind, and eyes of the Lord. He can and will heal our broken perspectives of self. How we got here, is not as important as our acknowledgement that we are here. Realization, opens the door to healing.

Arise Woman of Worth. Arise.

Chapter Two
Dressed Up and Pissed Off

"Let all bitterness and wrath and anger and clamor [perpetual animosity, resentment, strife, fault-finding] and slander be put away from you, along with every kind of malice [all spitefulness, verbal abuse, malevolence]." - *Ephesians 4:13*

I have always known how to dress well. Basically, growing up in the Favors' household, it was impossible not to. My parents were the best dressed adults I knew.

Well, my aunties knew how to slay too. Aunt Dot and Aunt Elaine, you two created your own lanes of dressing well. Rest on my Queens, I will always love you two.

My mother was so classy. She was sharp. She wore her heels, pearls, diamonds, and top elegant apparel, every time. She shopped at many nice stores and knew how to find a bargain. Mama taught me the ins and outs of bargain shopping. She schooled me early.

My Queen was so put together, so regal, so clean. Dressed to a tee, was my Woman of Worth, every time she hit the scene. She was the epitome of a DIVA, minus the attitude, of course.

What made my mother most beautiful to me was beautiful heart, contagious smile, and warm and loving eyes. What she seemed to accentuate, was her outside.

Taking many cues from her, I learned how to cover up my pain, with the perfect amount of concealer, blush, and lip stain. Yet, she had one saying, that in my heart remains. She taught me, "Pretty is as pretty does."

I learned to pray, *God please make my heart pretty.*

My father was the same way. He was super-fly. He donned diamonds on the pinky fingers. Perfectly shined gold, draped around his neck. The latest in fashion, leather coats, boots, or shoes. He sported tailored jackets, pants, or suits.

He strutted with the utmost in confidence, pride, and swag. I wanted to marry a man just like him some day. Would I?

Mama was sharp. Daddy was sharp. So of course, they raised a daughter that was…sharp. You see, we mastered dressing up the outside of our bodies to perfection.

What we never seemed to quite get, was how to dress up our confused, hurting, and angry hearts. This is where we needed the Savior.

I did not really know that I had so much anger, until God started dealing with *me* over the past year. I would look at my sons, and think, *"They must get that spirit of anger from their fathers."* Yes, I said *fathers.*

Then, my little granddaughter started flipping out and having temper tantrums, *well* before she turned one. It is as if the Holy Spirit was saying, "Who are you going to blame this on Twila?" I had to come to the realization that I had issues.

I was the common denominator in my children's and granddaughter's lives. I had to lay out on my face, before God, and pray for Him to deliver me and my seed from this spirit of anger. It all began with self -recognition. God was saying, "Twila, where are you?"

I was the queen at the Masquerade Ball. I remember hearing a song by Minister Tonya Baker called *Masquerade,* that arrested my soul. The jig was up. Like, how dare the Lord use her to call me out like this?

(Smile Tonya.)

Baby Listen. I had to really face some things about myself, my marriage, and my situation. I did not take my mask all the way off in 2002 though. I just downsized.

Instead of wearing a full mask, I wore more of a Fascinator styled mask. I was now willing to reveal more of myself, just not the parts too painful to face within. Here are a few reasons why wearing masks are stumbling blocks:

1. They keep you from showing up as your authentic self.
2. Masks keep you trapped in your pain.
3. They delay your healing.
4. They block you from receiving the love of others.
5. They block you from giving love to other people

My mask wearing did not come to a complete end until, God required me this book to pen. Now, I am finally free.

We need to be real with God. God knows E-V-E-R-Y-T-H-I-N-G! Why hide from Him? Doing so, just delays our deliverance. Look, eventually we can get to a place of pain, when we will strip down in front of everybody and scream, "Right here God! It hurts right here."

How about we allow God to deliver us from ourselves, our anger, and whatever else is a stumbling block in our lives, before it gets to that point.

Remember Adam in the Garden of Eden? God asked Adam where he was, not because, the Omniscient (all seeing), God did not see and know where Adam was. He asked Adam where he was, because God wanted Adam to come to his senses and realize that he needed help.

"Then the LORD God called to the man, and said to him, "Where are you?" – Genesis 3:9

Is God calling your name? He has not lost you. Is it possible that you have lost God? For goodness sake, answer the call and get your behind some help.

I am a woman with issues. As you read my story, find hope. God specializes in women with Issues. I am living proof.

Are you still upset with God, over things that He allowed to happen to you as a child? Many people are. If so, you might as well get real with God and tell Him how you feel. He is not afraid of your emotions.

The only one you are harming, by trying to keep them bottled up, is yourself.

It is hard to walk out your full potential, when you are still fighting the demons from your past.

It is nearly impossible to stroll as a Queen, when you are rocking with a Princess mentality.

I will disclose some of the pain and trauma I had hidden, deeply within the recesses of my heart and mind, in just a moment. First, I want to know if you can relate to playing Dress Up.

Reflections

Now stop and quiet yourself. Turn of your cellphone, tv, and music. Pray, and sit quietly for a response from the Holy Spirit.

What are you hiding from?

_____

_____

_____

_____

_____

_____

Who are you Hiding From?

_____

_____

_____

_____

_____

_____

God, we come before you as humbly as we know how. We stand before you, naked. Take us and make us over Lord. Heal us and make us whole.

We no longer hide from you. We may not be at a place where we are standing boldly before your throne. However, we are here. You know what we need. Please be it, do it, and bless us with it. In the name of Jesus, we pray, Amen.

Chapter Three
Playing Dress Up

"Search me, O God, and know my heart;
test me and know my anxious thoughts." Psalms
139:23 NLT

Have you ever just wanted to cry and express how you really feel? I have often said, if I could throw myself out on the floor and cry and scream, like Kayla does on occasion, it would feel so good. I was so tired of being grown up sometimes. However, I don't get to take this off.

You know, I am often the screaming, crying nine-year-old, that hurts. I get scared. I want my Mama. I want my Daddy too. Yet, I must put on a brave face, like I got it all together, who is there for me when I don't have it together?

I often wondered, does anyone care enough to recognize that I am having a Dress up kind of day? You all know, it is that kind of day where you put on the Grown-up clothes, makeup, and shoes.

You show up at work, church, and home, but for real, you have on a zip up blanket sleeper, holding your favorite doll, and sucking your thumb.

Who encourages the encourager, the minister, the author? God does. Look to God. Pray to Him.

I will lift up my eyes to the hills—
From whence comes my help?
My help comes from the Lord,
Who made heaven and earth. – Psalms 121: 1-2

Do you remember playing Dress Up as a little kid? It was always, so much fun. My mother's wardrobe was beast, so I had a ball playing dress up.

I would put on her pearls, oversized bracelets, and 6-inch heels. Then, prance around and look in the mirror, imagining that I was all *grown up.*

We would look in the mirror and just grin, as we imagine being a grown up like them. The amazing thing about playing like you were a grown up back then was, we could give our parents back their stuff.

We could laugh and giggle, and after handing them their pearls, shoes, hats, and clothes, back, we could run off and be carefree children again.

"When I was a child, I spoke like a child, I thought like a child, I reasoned like a child; when I became an adult, I put an end to childish ways." 1 Corinthians 13:11 NRSV

Being in our twenties, thirties, forties, and beyond, it does not work like that. As adults, we have to keep our suits on. We do not get to revert back to being carefree children again.

We have to play grown up. Even when, the scared little girl is the one that wakes up in the morning, and you need her to be the strong woman of faith.

Lord, what do we do when society requires us to make quick decisions, be grown, act grown, and keep it moving as if we are super humans, unaffected by anything.

How do we heal in a flawed church institution, where any sign of sickness or crying out is misconstrued as having weak faith, or being demon possessed?

We desire to put away childish things, but where exactly do we put them? Who exactly, is available to help us with this thing called adulthood?

Our insecurities, temper tantrums, indecisiveness, and self-indulgent ways, very much resemble that of a child's. Yet, our anointing, callings, gifting, and cravings, are that of an adult.

Our cognitive aptitude may be that of a genius, while our emotional maturity may have arrested at the age we were molested.

Many times, we present as CEO'S with the emotional intelligence of a nine or twelve-year-old. *God heal us, and make us whole.*

God, we are tired of playing Double Dutch. *Make us one Lord. Please, in Jesus' Name, Amen.*

This is exactly why we need God to heal us of ALL our issues. God does not want us walking around as scared little children in grown up clothes. For He did not give us a spirit of fear, that is from Satan.

"For God has not given us a spirit of fear, but of power and of love and of a sound mind." 2 Timothy 5:7

It is necessary for us to pray fervently for our power, love, and sound mind. If God said I can have it, I want it ALL. How about you?

I did not recognize that little girl was hanging around inside of me, until I started this writing journey. Now I can say, God heal her too. She deserves a chance to appreciate her worth, and blossom within.

God will take the trembling child inside of us, and integrate them with the mature Christian that we are. It is necessary that we become one, because a double minded person is unstable in all their ways.

It is okay to say, "Daddy, I am scared." This is my prayer to God many times. Your fear does not catch God by surprise. He is all knowing. He has been dealing with folks like us, since the beginning of humankind. Literally.

I once heard a preacher say, "there is a scripture for fear for each day of the year." (I guess you double back during Leap year.) Look, why would God need to breathe so many anti-scare scriptures in the Bible, if He did not know we would face fear sometimes. Got it?

Ask God to show you the root of the fear. Is it from something from your past? Is it over something real or imagined? Pray for an action plan to overcome your fear. Follow through.

This is where we get shaky. Our follow through is horrible. We want God to give us a quick fix for our fears and emotional issues. Whereas, God most often wants us to do some work.

It is hard to feel like a Queen, when you feel afraid and all out of sorts. The blessing is, you do not lose your worth when you face trials and tribulations. It belongs to you. It resides within you.

It is harder to stand boldly, when you are bowed over with timidity and anxiety. I have dealt with anxiety since I was at least nine years old. It is a peace wrecker.

My mother said I was a worry wort as a child. It was not by choice.

Fear, anxiety, and timidity are joy and peace stealers.

God can give us peace from them all.

God can surely heal people instantaneously, of anything He wants to. He is Jehovah Rapha-The God Who heals.

He is the Great and Mighty God. He has healed my son instantaneously, Hallelujah!

I have seen Him perform this amazing miracle, right before my very eyes. My son's faith made him well. If there was another chapter being written in the Bible today, my son would have his own chapter.

I do not add this to boast on my son, *at all*.

I want to encourage you, in this very hour, to trust God!

Miracles did not only happen in the "Bible Days," they are happening, right now! Good God Almighty!!!

Trust God, with all your heart!!!

God delivered me from postpartum psychosis, in an instance. Women have killed their children with this diagnosis. God kept His hands on me and my babies. You cannot tell me my God is not a miracle working God!!!

Seek Him while He can be found!!!

It is not always spooky deep. It may be as simple as getting your behind some counseling. Pick up the phone and schedule an appointment to meet with your bishop or pastor.

It is very likely, that talking to someone will help you so much more than you know. I have been there. I know what it is like trying to keep bottled up emotions in, to the point of being about to explode.

Beloved, that is so unhealthy. For me, I experienced horrible dreams, migraines, stomach pains, anxiety, and frequent crying spells. This is not the will of God for our lives.

Pray and ask God for *wisdom* about who to talk to. Everyone is not capable of handling your pain. However, God is faithful. IF you listen to Him and use discernment, He will lead you to a pastor, therapist, or solid person, whose shoulder you can depend.

"If you need wisdom, ask our generous God, and he will give it to you. He will not rebuke you for asking." James 1:5 NLT

Many of the pastors and bishops you sit under can give you wise counsel. Many. However, again pray and use discernment. If they are shady on Sunday mornings, they are not going to suddenly, become sound pastoral counselors throughout the week, unless God does the miraculous. Try the spirit, by the Spirit.

"Beloved, do not believe every spirit, but test the spirits, whether they are of God; because many false prophets have gone out into the world"- 1 John 4: 1

Having someone to give you sound spiritual advice and pray with you may bring about the healing you need.

I have seen situations, where the combination of both spiritual and psychological counseling has been of great benefit.

Make a decision not to limit God on His methods of healing you, and you will decide to heal well.

"If you need wisdom, ask our generous God, and he will give it to you. He will not rebuke you for asking." James 1:5 NLT

Better is coming, blessed man of worth and woman of worth. Better is coming. Just don't give up. God is our Healer. He is Jehovah Rapha.

Without God, I would not be alive today. I thank Him and praise Him for my life. Every second I am on this earth, is precious to me. I know, that it is only by His grace and mercy that I am here, in my right mind.

Chapter Four
GOD IS THE GREAT PHYSICIAN

"O Lord my God,
I cried to You for help, and You healed me." - Psalms
30:2 NASB

 He is able and willing to heal us, everywhere we hurt. Are you willing to be vulnerable enough to show him your pain?

Will you bear your heart, before the Lord?

Are you at a point in your life where you are like look God, I am tired of living the dual reality of scared child and brave adult, heal me and make me whole?

If so, cry out to God to help you, and keep reading.

God loves you! He is not going to leave you alone.

He promises to be with us. You can bank on His word.

"Be strong and of good courage, do not fear nor be
afraid of them; for the Lord your God, He is the One who

goes with you. He will not leave you nor forsake you."
Deuteronomy 31:6

Reflections

Take a Moment and Talk to God, in Your Own Way. Ask Him to heal the little girl or boy that resides within.

God desires to heal every part of you. Even, the inner child. Most of us have one.

_____

_____

_____

_____

_____

_____

_____

_____

_____

_____

_____

_____

Prayer,

God, please redeem the time for us. Bless us with double for our trouble. Lord give us double portions of peace, hope, joy, and love. Help us to focus on You and not the people that caused us pain.

Lord help us to be of one mind and of one accord within ourselves. Help us to not be double minded. Heal everything that is broken in us and makes us whole again Father. Make us, know You like never before. Help us to walk closer to You than we ever have before.

Bless to fall in love with the character of who You are. Forgive us Lord, for calling on You, only when we need something. Help us to grow to call You just to say how much we love and appreciate you God. These and all things, I pray in the name of Jesus,

Amen

Chapter Five
We Don't Have to Be Tough

Here is the thing, as you get into my story, you might cry. If you are a brother and need a man hug, it is okay (smile.) This is a complete, no judgement zone.

Look, life is hard. I do not care how saved you are, sometimes life sucks. Let me be clear, I prefer life over the alternative, Amen? Amen.

When we feel weak, it is all good. God picks up the slack. It is very difficult to carry the weight of our past hurts and pains. Give them over to God.

One way to get some of that burden off your back is to simply, open up and finally talk to God about it.

You have been trying to avoid dealing with your issues on your own. The struggle is over.

Your helper is here. Meet Christ.

And He said to me, "My grace is sufficient for you, for My strength is made perfect in weakness." Therefore, most gladly I will rather boast in my infirmities, that the power of Christ may rest upon me. -2 Corinthians 12:9

Society has taught us that we must be tough. That is why so many of us are walking around a hot mess. We try to keep up this façade of being hard, while in reality, we are falling apart on the inside.

Beloved, you have to be real enough with yourself to expose the real you. You must get in touch with your real fears, hurts, thoughts, hang-ups, stinking thinking, and issues, before you can lay them out on the table before God.

In fact, you can go before God and say, "God, look, I don't know exactly what is going on with me, but I know I need your help." Listen here, God will do the rest. He does not require your permission to help you. He does like it though. He is a Gentleman.

Recognition, that we have an issue, assists us with breaking though the barriers of pride and denial. Once we knock those walls down, we can be more vulnerable before God and ask Him for the help we need

After being so exhausted, from trying to heal myself, I eventually found myself coming to God, saying, "*Here I am God, please do whatever You need to make me right.*"

God's promise to us is His all sufficient grace. This is a fancy way of saying, God's grace is more than enough for whatever we are going through.

Excuse my language right here, but, "Ain't that good news?!

Chapter Six
We are Not Alone!

"and lo, I am with you always, even to the end of the age."

-Matthew 28:20 NASB

There have been many times I have felt so alone. I have been alone physically throughout this writing process. I have cried so many days and nights.

God would send His Sweet Holy Spirit to comfort me.

Now, I will be honest, there were some nights I was hoping for someone about 6'4, with a nice caramel complexion (smile)....

Anyway, the Holy Spirit came through as my Comforter, every single time. He is faithful. I am so grateful for His love and steadfastness in my life.

As we recall events from our youth, it is hard to imagine that God was there. It is hard to fathom how God could be present at the same time, in the same room, when someone was harming me, yet allowed it.

Yet, He was. He is all places, always. This is very difficult to sit in. There is no cute cliché' to fix this one. This is a harsh reality every Christian must face, who has dealt with any type of abuse, loss, or hardship.

It would be easier to cope with being hurt, if we knew God had taken a sick day. However, to know that an all seeing, all powerful, ever present God, permitted my tragedy, took me a very long time to stop being angry about. Honestly, it was hard to admit that I was pissed at God. I then, had to pray to the God I was angry with, to show me how to forgive him. You know what? He loves me so much, He did just that.

I hope you are getting this today. You can be honest with God about how you feel towards Him. He knows anyway. He just wants you to open your mouth and talk to Him.

Chapter Seven
God Is Bigger Than Your Emotions

Guess what? You might as well get real with God and admit that you are upset, angry, and disappointed too. God already knows your heart towards Him. WE can't hide our heart from God. It is honesty and truth that God desires from us. We must show God where we hurt. It is when we become naked before Him, that our best healing takes place.

You need to show the GREAT PHYSICIAN, everywhere you hurt in, order to receive complete restoration. How honest are you willing to be before God? Have you fully undressed before Him and showed him your angry heart? It is extremely uncomfortable, but necessary.

It is when we can admit out anger towards God, that He can heal us of this anger. Did you all just read this?! The same God that we are angry at, can heal of us of this very emotion. WHO couldn't serve a God like this?

I had to come to a place of admitting my feelings towards God. It was at THAT POINT, that He started my process of healing from the wounds.

God needs to restore your heart of stone with a heart of flesh. I am speaking as one, who has undergone a fresh heart transplant.

Chapter Eight
A New Heart

I remember going to see my primary physician about twelve years ago. She read my list of ailments. There were at least seven on there. She went down and checked off each ailment and said, "stress related, stress related..."

Some of the stress was from external stressors going on in my life. I am certain, that most of my stress was coming from the disharmony and unrest I had within.

I wanted to say a quick prayer, recite a scripture, and call myself healed. God required me to bare my heart to Him, so that He could remove the stony places.

I will give you a new heart and put a new spirit within you; I will take the heart of stone out of your flesh and give you a heart of flesh. -Ezekiel 36:26

I had to trust Him to remove the callouses. They were just tough places, with decreased *blood* flow.

God needed to do a spiritual coronary artery bypass graft. The surgeon needed to reattach my blocked vessels to a new heart, so the Blood of Jesus could flow effectively through me, to give me my life back.

You and I will live life abundantly without the fear of man. Jesus came so that we can do just that. It is the devil that wants us worn, depressed, and suffering. He wants to steal our joy, peace, and hope.

I don't know about you, but I am going to be about living the abundant life for the rest of my days. I want what Jesus wants for me. I have learned that I do not aim high enough with my desires.

I give God this wimpy prayer list like, Lord please make my life good, Amen.

He is like, "Good? Wait do you know who I am? I am the Great I AM! Why would I stop at giving you a good life, when I have already paved the way for you to have so much better?"

Beloved, are you willing to submit to the process of God? Are you ready to receive a new heart and new spirit from Him? I hope so.

"Where can I go from Your Spirit?
Or where can I flee from Your presence?
 If I ascend into heaven, you *are* there;
If I make my bed in hell, behold, you *are there."_ Psalms
139: 7-8*

God has your back. He will heal you where you hurt.
Tell the truth. Admit to Him you are in pain.

Show the Lord, the you that you hide from everyone
else. Reveal to Him, the heart you keep at bay from
those around you. Your loving Father has just what you
need to make you whole. It is not too late. He has just the
right healing balm for your wounds. There is a balm in
Gilead.

"Is there no balm in Gilead,
Is there no physician there?
Why then is there no recovery
For the health of the daughter of my people?" –
Jeremiah 8:22

Chapter Nine
You Can Touch My Wounds

"And they overcame him by the BLOOD of the LAMB and by the WORD OF THEIR TESTIMONY,"-Revelation 12:11

So listen, everything is not deep. Oftentimes, we want babies in Christ and even nonbelievers to come running to the alter, and believing in a God they cannot see, simply because we preached a "powerful word from the Lord."

People are looking at you like, "Who *are you? How can we know this God you preach about is real, if we don't know that you are real? How can I schedule a meeting with you to tell you my dirt, when you come across as so perfect and distant?"*

I say to you, come, read, and touch my wounds.

Chapter Ten
Look, I Need to Put My Finger in It

When you have been through some things, you just need to know, that you know it is God. Maybe, I am the only one. If so, that is cool.

I have my moments where it is like, "God I believe you and I thank you in advance." Other times, man listen, I am like Doubting Thomas, "God *if* this is You, I need a sign, let me put my finger on it."

Don't sit up here and act like you all don't have your moments. '*God if this job is for me, let them call me at precisely 3:00 PM and offer me $ 75,000, and my start day be on November 15th Lord Jesus, then I will know, that I know it is you.* Then, for good measure we will throw in, '*Lord I just trust you. In the matchless, faithful, come through-fullness…name of Jesus I pray, Amen Lord Jesus, thank you so much…And so it is!'*

"So, he said to them, "Unless I see in His hands the print of the nails, and put my finger into the print of the nails, and put my hand into His side, I will not believe."

And after eight days, His disciples were again inside, and Thomas with them. Jesus came, the doors being shut, and stood in the midst, and said, "Peace to you!" Then, He said to Thomas, "Reach your finger here, and look at My hands; and reach your hand here, and put it into My side. Do not be unbelieving, but believing."

And Thomas answered and said to Him, "My Lord and my God!"

Jesus said to him, "Thomas because you have seen Me, you have believed. Blessed are those who have not seen and yet have believed."-John 20:25-29

IF JESUS-THE MESSIAH, THE SON OF THE LIVING GOD, THE ROSE OF SHARON, THE GOOD SHEPHERD, THE WAY, THE TRUTH, AND THE LIFE, - GOD WRAPPED IN FLESH Y'ALL, could be caring enough, to be transparent enough, to show Thomas where *HE hurt,* who on earth are we to be too uptight to show others our pain?

Who do we think we are? Are we higher than God? Have we become more relevant in ministry to think, "It doesn't take all that?" God forbid.

People need to know that we are real. There are people who have been bamboozled by scripture quoting, tongue speaking, word preaching devils. They are churched out. They need to put their fingers in our sides, to see if we are real.

If you are going to call yourself a minister, you are going to have to undress before the people and show them where you hurt. Jesus provided us with the most beautiful example of this-HIMSELF.

There are too many people walking around wounded, because they cannot find someone to tell them, they are not alone.

As preachers, want to pump people to try Jesus, without telling them *why* the need to. Trust me, the threat of Hell is not enough to convince a hurting world that they need a Savior. People have lost respect for the office of pastor, bishop, and religious leader, with good reason.

Many leaders have proven to be devils behind the pulpit. Many preachers have been nothing more than scripture quoting pimps.

For those of us who are truly called by God, to bring the hurting and lost sheep to Him, we better pull up our dresses, to reveal our sides, and show them where we were pierced.

We don't have time for pride. This is not the time to debate with people. In the name of Jesus, get over yourselves, and show them where you hurt. Make Jesus reachable for them. STOP ACTING LIKE YOU HAVE ARRIVED PASTORS AND LEADERS.

Get your behind on the alter with your congregants. Show them, you have wounds too. Let them know, you bleed too. I remember, feeling hopeless after hearing some preachers preach. I remember, walking out of church services feeling defeated, like, well I will never be as good as the pastor, so I might as well keep sinning.

Is this really the message God wants us preaching to HIS people?

People are debating, whether to jump off ledges, or live; and whether to slit their throats, or try again. They often don't want to hear another 3 points to a sermon.

God's people are desperate for a breakthrough. Will you take off your masks and help them? I will. You can touch my wounds. I bleed. I cry. I get it wrong a lot of times. But baby, I have a heart for God. I love Him, and He loves me back.

He does not need me to be perfect, He needs me to be authentic.

"for the LORD has sought out a man after his own heart. The LORD has already appointed him to be the leader of his people" – 1 Samuel 13:14

This passage refers to David being appointed King and being a man after God's own heart. You all know David, right? Church folk would say, "but he has a past." So, what? Our pasts cannot abort out destinies. David was a worshipper. God loved him *still.*

I have *no doubt* that my name is all up in this text. Twila is a woman after God's own heart. I cannot afford, not to show you my wounds Thomas and Thomassina.

God has been too good to me. Come see a Man.

Even in our imperfection, we are the closest thing to Jesus that they will see on earth. They need Jesus. However, they need to see Him through you.

Are you willing to humble yourselves and serve them?

Like Doubting Thomas, they need to feel our wounds to know we are real. We must be transparent enough to show them. I was from the show me state too.

I needed to see and feel your scars, to believe that you were ever hurt.

If you are in leadership and reading this book, please allow God to make you vulnerable enough to show others your scars.

This takes nothing away from your healing, nor the God that healed you and made you whole. Transparency, simply makes us human and relatable. It gives others hope.

If I tell someone hey, I heard Jesus can heal a broken heart, they may nod, say, "ok," and keep it moving. If I say to this same person, "Hey, it looks like you are having a hard time. Can I share with you how God helped me when my heart was broken? Which leader do you think a broken person will listen to?

It is one thing to tell someone of a Jesus that can. It is far more powerful, to share your story with someone, and tell them of the Jesus that will.

People of God, show people your scars. They need to feel you. When I was a dead woman walking, I was not interested in a minister's pedigree. I wanted to know, "Do you care enough for me, to speak life to my bleeding heart?"

Man, and woman of God, it is time out for your pride. Undress, or be exposed. The choice is yours. Shepherd, how dare you let your sheep wallow in despair, when you hold the key to their deliverance, but don't want to drop your façade?

"Pride goes before destruction,

and haughtiness before a fall." Proverbs 16:18 NLT

Chapter Eleven
Keeping it Real

I have been through so much. I do not have the space or desire to tell you everything I have gone through. We would all need intensive therapy if I did that.

I will share, as the Holy Spirit leads me.

I had to start somewhere, so I started with my first trauma. I did not think it bothered me much. That is, until the Lord had me write about it, and examine my life.

The blessing is, I survived! God turned my tests into my testimony. He turned my trials into my triumphs. Before I can shout though, I have to deal with it. He is perpetually restoring me, and reassuring me that I have worth. As a matter of fact, I can go on and shout right now, because, I am still here-He turned it!

Man, and Woman of God, you are valuable to God, no matter what. It is the *no matter what,* that most of us wrestle with. *You* are the Apple of His eye! When God looks at you, He sees Himself. He sees His original design. Much like, we see our children as beautiful, no matter what they have done. God sees you as His original design and nothing less.

*"For thus says the L*ORD *of hosts: "He sent Me after glory, to the nations which plunder you; for he who touches you touches the apple of His eye.' – Zechariah 2:8*

I suffered abuse, at the hands of another person, growing up. It was hard for me to understand that his crime, did not erase my worth. If you endured any form or hurt, harm, or mistreatment, you did not lose your worth either.

Beloved, even if your innocence was distorted, your worth could never be taken from you. It was given to you from God. You are fearfully and wonderfully made. There are simply no conditions on that.

The word "are" is an absolute verb. There is no changing. Man, and woman of God, I pray that you get this in your spirit. You ARE fearfully and wonderfully made, you ARE a marvelous work of God.

As a matter of fact, so am I.

You are beautiful. You are fierce. You are still the apple of His eye. You are ENOUGH!

God please help us to see ourselves as beautifully and unstained as you see us, in the name of Jesus I pray, Amen.

Chapter Twelve
The Thief Came

The thief comes but to steal, kill, and destroy,"-John 10:10a

The enemy set so many traps to not just hurt me, but to destroy me. Some of them I discerned, and some I did not. However, God is greater. His plans for my life, shall come to pass.

When I was nine years old, I had not learned that people were bad. I had spent most of my time with my parents, who always treated me very well. I was the apple of their eyes.

Raised as an only child, although I had older brothers, I pretty much had mama and daddy's undivided attention as a young child.

I believed people where good. That had been my experience with people, so it was my frame of reference.

Of course, I had gotten the "Don't talk to strangers talk." I just did not take that talk to heart.

I often wonder how my life would have ended up, had it not been interrupted by a man that had his lustful desires in mind, instead of my best interest. I was robbed of my childlike wonder and innocence.

Chapter Thirteen
The New Girl on the Block

"Be sober, be vigilant; because your adversary the devil walks about like a roaring lion, seeking whom he may devour." 1 Peter 5:8

When I was nine years old, I met a friend named Yvette. She had recently moved into the neighborhood with her family.

I remember the exact day I met a girl, whose family would change my life. I was sitting on the steps of my Aunt Martha's house, on Cambridge Ave. in Dayton, Ohio. I played with my dolls alone, as I was accustomed to doing.

I noticed a girl that seemed a little older than me, holding the hand of a boy that was younger than me. She walked past me at least twice saying, "Well Mitchell, now that we moved over here, we don't' have *any* friends." I would later learn that Mitchell was the girl's younger brother.

The thing is, even at the age of nine, I was intuitive as heck. I knew she was baiting me to talk to her. Had I known the trap Satan had laid, just ahead for me, I would have just ignored those hints.

I bit the hook. In part, so she could shut the heck up, and the other part out of sympathy. There was a little hint of curiosity there too. I would later regret the bite. She was not the problem. Yvette seemed to be cool.

I would excitedly ask my parents for permission to go and play over Yvette's house. In a short matter of time, my parents would set up a meeting with her folks.

They talked about whatever grown folks talk about. I don't know, *how in the heck* Mr. Wilcox did not make the hairs on the back of their neck stand up. However, he slipped under the radar.

I was given permission to play with my new friend. I was so happy! I liked going over to the Wilcox's house. Yvette and I just fell into easy conversation.

Yvette and her mother introduced me to Gospel Music. I was hooked! My parents even allowed me to go with Mrs. Wilcox to a few Quartet Gospel concerts, after church on Sundays. I was in Heaven.

Chapter Fourteen
Something Just Ain't Right

"For to one is given the word of wisdom through the Spirit, to another the word of knowledge through the same Spirit, to another faith by the same Spirit, to another gifts of healings by the same Spirit, to another the working of miracles, to another prophecy, to another discerning of spirits,"- 1 Corinthians 12: 9-10

Even as a little girl, I had discernment. God gives babies discernment. They have by far, the keenest discernment on the planet. It is unbiased. This is why, it's of utmost importance not to force infants and toddlers into the arms of people they detect are not okay. In doing so, you are unknowingly conditioning them to override their God given gift of instinct.

Watching Kayla read people, over this past almost two years of her life, has blessed me tremendously. The girl is on point with her spiritual discernment. It has also served as a reminder of how awesome God is, to knit such a warning system into each one of His delicate creations, before one breathed our first breaths of life.

The more time I would spend over at Yvette's house, the more I started feeling like something was off about her father. I could not put my finger on it, but something about him made me feel uneasy. He was like that one uncle, that looked at you just a little too long.

I had never felt this way about any other person I had met. Well, the boys in the alley that tried to get me to take my panties down when I was four, made me feel uneasy, but other than them losers, no one else.

I knew enough to watch him, out of the corner of my eye, when I went over at Yvette's house to play. I just did not know enough to avoid going over to their house all together. I was nine.

After a few more trips around the block, the best advice I can give anyone is to ALWAYS PAY ATTENTION TO YOUR INSTINCT. ALWAYS.

God gives you that gut feeling for a reason. It is called spiritual discernment. In the Nursing field we simply say, "Trust your gut." DISCERNMENT DOES NOT LIE.

Chapter Fifteen
I Was So Confused

One summer day, I half walked, and half ran up the street to go and see my girl. I was so excited! I was imagining all of the fun Yvette and I were about to have. Maybe, we would go hang out at Princeton Park or something that day.

I had on this cute little pink halter top Mama had bought me. It was one of those halter tops that fully covered my front and tied up in the back.

I can't really remember what bottoms I put with it. Likely, some jean or white shorts. Fashion always mattered in my world, so I know it was something cute.

This particular day, instead of Yvette answering the door, like I had anticipated, her father did. He had this weird expression on his face.

Like this sly grin. Yuck, I just had a flashback of it as I am writing this story. Lord help me. My stomach still turns.

Now this man was tall, for real. He may have easily been six feet five inches. So, my short nine-year-old self, was trying to peer around him to search for Yvette.

He was like, "Hi, if you want to see her, you have to give me a kiss." I stepped back, like is this negro for real?

I snapped my neck back and said, "Wait what?" He said, "You heard me. If you want to see Yvette, you have to kiss me first." I thought, "This nasty creep." I felt a lot of different emotions, most of which I could not put into words.

I was baffled. This was off my radar. I didn't even like boys yet, let alone OLD NASTY MEN. I hesitated. Looked up the stairs, where my friend was.

Looked up at him as he blocked the stairs and thought, what the heck? I pecked him on the lips. My insides curled. I felt like I was going to hurl. My reward was getting to hang with my friend.

This was too high a price to pay.

The kisses turned in to him groping and pinching, my barely budding breast. I had no feeling in them. This was not wanted touch, AT ALL.

I was only nine years old. There I stood, paying a price that I could not afford. I was a BABY! I was VIOLATED,

SCARED, and CONFUSED. I was angry, humiliated, and hurt.

I looked up to her father as another father figure. He was everything BUT that to me. I had no frame of reference for this.

Mr. Wilcox was the beginning of the end of my healthy view of men. He never got inside of my panties, Thank God! He didn't need to though.

Unbeknownst to me, this pervert had gotten into my psyche. He was the first of many men that would confess loving God, but demonstrate behaviors that suggest otherwise.

Chapter Sixteen
Daddy Please Help Me

I always say, my father was my Superman. I literally thought he was a Superhero. I believed there was nothing he could not do. I always felt like the safest girl in the world in his presence. I was in love with my Daddy. He was literally, my first crush.

I think every little girl falls in love with her Daddy. My Daddy was handsome, strong, fun, rich, funny, smarty, cool, and the list went on and on. I was sure he would be able to fix whatever was broken inside of me and making me feel so off balanced, after being *touched* by my friend's father.

I ran home and told my parents what Mr. Wilcox did to me. I was so scared. I feared what had just happened. I was scared to tell my parents. I felt bad for Yvette, because I was pretty sure she was not going to have a Dad anymore.

I was petrified about my Daddy going to jail after he killed Mr. Wilcox. My imagination was on tilt. I could see the police taking Daddy off in hand cuffs. Me and Mama would be standing at the door with tears streaming down our cheeks screaming, "No officer. Please don't take him to jail. You don't understand."

Daddy would look back at me, with a longing stare. He would try to reassure me, that it would all be okay now. Mr. Wilcox would never hurt me again. Although, he had to go to the police station to straighten things out, he had killed the monster that hurt his daughter. I never had to be afraid again."

Chapter Seventeen
Wait No Police?

There were no police involved, at all.

Surprisingly, not much seemed to change. Of course, I was glad that my father did not commit murder. I was also kind of relieved that my offender was not dead.

It just seems like something should have been done to him. *Something.* Were adults allowed to hurt girls and get away with it? In retrospect, I guess I felt like no one defended my honor.

Clearly, a *convincing conversation* was held though. Mr. Wilcox never in life, touched me again. However, this was rather anticlimactic even for a nine-year-old.

I may have been a child, but I was smart enough to know, this creep had broken a few laws. I knew he had crossed the line. I just did not have the proper terminology for it.

What I did not perceive, nor do I remember hearing from anyone around me, was that I was precious, fearfully, or wonderfully made.

I have no recollection of hearing the words, "You have a right to be protected and safe." Something began to brew right beneath the surface. It was called rage.

Because I was unfamiliar with it, and had no outlet for it, I stuffed it back to stifle it's screams.

The cycle became vicious. The more he complained about my weight, the more my feelings were hurt. The more my feelings were hurt, the more I ate.

Wait, you think I am fat? I could not cope with the idea of the man who I looked up to like Superman, and loved with all my heart, calling me fat.

For the first time in my entire life, I felt like I was not pretty. I felt like I was not good enough. I felt ugly. I felt unwanted. I rejected.

These issues have followed me all my life. I am not saying it is because of my father.

They just have.

Now, I fight like Heck to reverse every negative tape and self-image that tries to bring me down.

Instead of recovering from my molestation and regaining my confidence as a girl, I seemed to be losing ground. I was slipping down into sadness.

God did not allow me to slip too far though. He gave me an unbelievably resilient spirit. I do not dare boast in my strength. It was ALL GOD.

"And He said to me, 'My grace is sufficient for you, for My strength is made perfect in weakness.' " -2 *Corinthians 12:9*

Chapter Eighteen
Five BIG Words

One of the unfortunate things about this whole scenario was, I don't remember hearing the words, "You *did not deserve this*." Those are five of the most powerful words in the universe.

I implore you to use them often, from a sincere place. If someone has the *courage* to tell you their story. Please, in the name of Jesus, validate them with these five words, YOU DID NOT DESERVE THIS.

Your words to them, may literally be the difference between them slitting their wrists, or seeking help.

Thankfully, Mama and I remained close. Daddy and I did too. I just had an attitude with the man that called me FAT.

In retrospect, I wonder if anyone made a connection between what they were seeing, and the dis-ease going on in my mind, heart, spirit, and soul?

I have no room to place blame. Lord knows, I missed so much as a parent with my children.

I would spend many years of my life yo-yo dieting and trying to get skinny, for a hand clap from Daddy.

You see, the first person I tried to please, was my Daddy.

My mother's love was unconditional, but my father's love, was performance and appearance based.

When I was nine, I had learned for the first time in my life, this thing called *shame*.

I was ashamed of my body. I can remember, trying to suck my stomach in when he was looking.

I just wanted to be loved, reassured---and now skinny.

This being a kid thing, was getting harder by the minute.

Unwanted touch was horrible. A strange man had molested my barely budding breasts. A familiar man had molested my barely budding self -image.

I wanted Daddy to love me and tell me I was okay.

Him telling me how much weight I gained, when my heart was ripping apart with pain, was more than I could bear.

How could my world, that had been so perfect, be turned upside-down? It literally felt like I was in a downward spiral, that I could not stop.

It is as if, I went to bed one night happy go lucky, and woke up the next day, sad as hell. I didn't have the courage to ask, but all I wanted to know was, *Daddy do you still love me?*

Chapter Nineteen
Take Time to Speak Life to Your Children

"Death and life are in the power of the tongue," -
Proverbs 18:21

I don't remember much reassurance coming from Mama or Daddy, to be honest. I do not remember hearing either one of my parents saying, "Twila you are so valuable to us and we are so sorry this happened to you."

They may have said it.
I just do not remember.

Chapter Twenty
I Was a Wounded Soul

I am not sure, whether I knew I had self-worth and value before I was molested. I am not certain these concepts were even heavily taught, back when I was a little girl.

What I am sure of, is I began to feel off balanced from this moment forward.

I felt unsure about my body. I was no longer sure that my body was just my own. In today's terms, I guess you would say, I had started having boundary issues.

During this same time frame, an older female relative of my next-door neighbor, had rubbed my budding breasts also. She said, she was, "helping me." Though I never asked for help.

My soul was hurting. I put myself in risky situations. My parents argued incessantly. I dressed up my outside, while trying to find my footing on the inside.

Words like "fat" and "black" were frequently hurled at my mother, from my father's lips during their arguments. Though, not intended for me, bullets have no names.

You see, while I was still trying to heal from molestation, and seek validation from my father, who could not see my inner turmoil, I discovered, he was having an affair on *us.*

I learned at an early age, that I could not trust the men from the outside or the inside. What was it about *me,* that made them treat *me* so badly?

Chapter Twenty-One
I Was Forced to Grow Up Too Fast

I would continue to be broken, with no concept of beautiful.

Hurting, confused, and angry, I sought to stop my pain. I was a good girl, with a hurting soul.

The tweens were horrible for me. Not only did I get molested, and have to adjust to my new identity as a fat girl, but I also discovered my father was cheating on my mother.

My peaceful home became a hostile battlefield, seemingly overnight. I was forced to grow up way too fast. In my child-like mind, I was trying to process concepts like molestation, infidelity, divorce, and who gets the child, AKA-me.

During my tweens, I balanced becoming a marriage counselor to my parents, and trying to heal as a child.

"When my father and my mother forsake me,
Then the Lord will take care of me."- Psalm 27:10

The Holy Spirit was there, whispering to me. My pain was louder than His whisper though.

As a child, I had not yet learned His voice and known to take heed to it.

What I did come to understand, is what abandonment felt like.

I did not perceive my worth then. Truthfully, I still struggle with underestimating my value and worth now.

Not realizing how amazingly valuable I was, along with having been molested, led me down a path of promiscuity as a teenager.

I also tried my hand at drinking. Fortunately, drinking was not really my thing.

I needed lidocaine, an anesthetic, for my broken spirit and soul. Mama tried her best to be there for me, despite her pain in the marriage.

I longed for my father's attention during my adolescence. He was there for me at times. He would weave and bob, in and out of emotional availability.

I acted out. The thing with acting out is, we may aim to hurt others, however, only we are left holding the bag, so to speak.

I desperately needed the love, affection, and attention I was not getting at home. Initially, I started sleeping with a few boys.

This led to a lifestyle of fornication, that left me feeling more worthless on the inside, than words can describe. However, the temporary satisfaction kept me chasing a feeling.

Brokenness and desperation for attention, often cloud good judgement. I was really a smart girl. I made some bad decisions though.

When I look back at the mess I dealt with, not to mention the messes I made, I have no choice but to Thank God. I realize, He was there all along. Even when I had no concept of Who He was, He was there.

So many times, if we never look back at our pasts, we want to convince everyone, including ourselves, that we have arrived. By doing so, we cannot address the brokenness and jacked up patterns we have.

I am not suggesting we go and pitch a tent, to dwell in our pasts. I am suggesting, that we go back and examine what makes us tick.

Do some self -examination.

When you find yourself repeating the same patterns, relationship after relationship, job after job, church after church, then the problem just might be you.

Give it over to God. This happened to you. It is not the definition of who you are.

You are a survivor. You are triumphant over what tried to label, oppress, and keep you down.

Reflection Time

Tell God about every hurt and pain this brought up for you. Ask Him what path He wants you to take for your breakthrough. Beloved, God desires to see you walking through life, FREE INDEED!

"For he who the Son sets free is free indeed."-John 8:36

_____

_____

_____

_____

_____

_____

_____

_____

_____

_____

_____

God please set us all Free in the name of Jesus I pray, Amen!

Prayer for All of Us

God, I pray that you heal and restore every man, woman, boy and girl that has been stripped of their innocence right now in the name of Jesus. Touch now Lord. God, if this book rips scabs off of healing wounds, I pray that it is only so you can heal the wounded areas completely.

Leave no area unhealed Lord. Soak us in Your healing balm, God until we ache no more. Replace our despair with hope. Gives us the oil of joy for our sorrow, beauty for our ashes, and a garment of praise for our spirit of heaviness.

God, if any unforgiveness remains in us for our abusers, God I ask that you help us forgive right now Lord. Set us free from the bondage of unforgiveness right now God.

Lord heal us of all the negative words that still resonate in our minds, hearts, and souls. Lord heal and deliver us from negative self-images and low self-esteem. These things are painful and crippling God. They prevent us from walking out our fullest potential in You Lord. God cast them down, in the MIGHTY NAME OF JESUS WE PRAY,

   AMEN!

Give the pain of your sexual abuse over to God. Ask Him to heal your mind, heart, muscle memory, and to remove every trigger that remains in you.

Seek professional help. Use every positive tool necessary, to live a triumphant life. You survived the worst part. Now do the work to be released from the prison that has kept you bound.

You are worth it man and woman of God. I was worth it. Sisters and Brothers, Arise! We have worth! The devil can't keep us down by what already happened to us, we are overcomers.

Jesus told us we would have trials and tribulation, but to be of good cheer, because, He has overcome the world! Chin up buttercup! We will recover all!

"I have told you all this so that you may have peace in me. Here on earth you will have many trials and sorrows. But take heart, because I have overcome the world."- John 16:33 NLT

Chapter Twenty-Two
There Is Purpose in Our Pain

Reliving my molestation hurt like crazy. I did not deserve this. No one ever deserves to be harmed. Not ever. God does not desire for any of His precious children to be harmed. He loves us to much for this.

Why He allows things like this to happen, I cannot answer this. Each one of us must make peace with the fact that we may never know the answer to this. It is important for our peace and for our sanity, to ask God to help us move past the "why God" phase, to the "what God" phase.

You can gain power in asking the crucial questions. "What do you want me to do with my story? Who do you want me to tell it to? How can I turn my pain to purpose?"

Had I stayed stuck in the Why God, I would have never allowed Him to use me to write this book. Allow God to flip your pain, for His good purpose. He's intentional.

Chapter Twenty-Three
Your Suffering Is Not in Vain

One of the biggest things that gives me strengths, is knowing that my suffering has not been in vain. I mean this thing. If my tears, can save another young woman from experiencing the pain I have endured, it was worth it.

As you continue to read my story, you will understand more about what I mean. You must find the purpose in your pain. Instead of getting stuck in the "Why me Lords?" Flip that thing.

Find strength and ask Him, "What now Lord?" I can't change the fact that "it" happened, now what do You want me to do with this? In doing this, you will find strength and power, through Christ.

You will become an active participant in your healing. You will find, and I am finding, the more we tell our stories, the more we realize we are survivors! We are strong, we are more than conquerors!

We are going to get our therapy, counseling, spiritual counseling, whatever it takes, and live.

Many of the most powerful and successful ministers I have listened to on Periscope and Facebook, or have talked to in person, have been through hell. Many still battle with depression, anxiety, self-doubt, bad memories, fear, you name it.

They are no different than me and you. We are all people on this earth. People have issues, period. Thank God, He specializes in people with issues. Come here woman, with the issue of blood.

How long will you allow your issues to hold you back? Someone is desperately waiting for you. My testimony won't reach them like yours will. Get up!

God has a way of using our deepest pain to catapult us into our most powerful ministries. No one can reach people that experience certain types of storms, like you and me.

And, let me just dispel this myth. I have heard so many preachers say, "God can't use you until you get fixed. Broken people can't minister to broken people."

Ma'am or Sir, have you ever opened your Bible? Now, if someone is mentally unstable, that is one thing.

However, if you mean someone who has issues, cannot be an effective witness, listen here, there would be no witnesses.

We are all storm walkers. Better yet, we are all storm survivors. What better man or woman, to grab our sister or brother, by the hand and say, come and see a Man?

No hardship is ever wasted in God.

"And we know that all things work together for good to those who love God, to those who are the called according to His purpose." – Romans 8:28

Reflection Time

Take Time and ask Daddy God What He Wants You to Do with the Pain You are Experiencing.

Chapter Twenty-Four
Call to Action for Parents and Guardians

"Children are a gift from the Lord; they are a reward from him. " Psalms 127:3 NLT

Lord, teach us how to take better care of our gifts.

My God, it is my prayer that as parents we are careful of the messages we are downloading into our children's brains. These words have the capability to give life or to destroy them. Give them life! Allow them to experience peace and joy.

By the way, this is for the duration of our lives. We are blessed to be able to love on our children and speak life to them as long as we shall live.

We may not have gotten right yesterday. It is okay. Ask God for forgiveness. Ask your children for forgiveness. The biggest person we need to forgive is ourselves.

My God help us to forgive ourselves for dropping our babies when they were young. Jesus, we are still beating ourselves down for allowing Junior to roll off the couch

when he was three months old, and he is twenty-three now.

Give us the ability to forgive ourselves in order to freely love our children now. Bless us to see the gems we have in front of us, and to soak up the opportunities You have given us NOW.

The Holy Spirit just revealed to me that we are not helping our children to the fullest of our ability right now, because we are still condemning ourselves for what we did not do before.

We cannot go back. We can only give them our best versions of ourselves now. *My God unchain us from the demon of regret and condemnation in the name of Jesus. Saturate us and revive us today with the life-giving power of the Blood of Jesus NOW GOD, in the mighty, matchless, infallible, name of Jesus Christ I pray, Amen*

"There is therefore now no condemnation to those who are in Christ Jesus," – Romans 8:1

Build your babies up. There are plenty people on the outside that will try to tear them down. They don't deserve to fight the enemy within and without their homes. The words you speak have no expiration date or delete function.

Speak Life into your child. Start today. It is necessary. You could save their lives. You could very well be the difference between them putting a gun to their head, or reaching out for help. I mean this thing.

Celebrate Small Successes. I do not care *how much* they may wreck your nerves. Find the one could thing your son or daughter did well every day, and celebrate them for it. It may seem silly to you, trust me, it is monumental to the child suffering with low self-worth.

Don't allow others to speak death on your children. Ladies, DO NOT stay with a man or lady that talks down to your children for the sake of not being lonely. Listen it is not worth it. I did that, and the effects are far reaching and never worth it.

Find Something! Find *something* to praise your child for even on the rough days. Even if it is screwing the top back on the tube of toothpaste, listen, and go ahead and make up a song for him or her.

Tell your gift from God, today and forever more that they ARE fearfully and wonderfully made because GOD SAID SO.

TEACH YOUR BABIES THEY ARE WORTH IT-THAT IS WHO THEY ARE. Breathe this into their spirits. BELOVED *YOU* ARE FEARFULLY AND WONDERFULLY MADE.

"For You have formed my inward parts; You have covered me in my mother's womb. I will praise You, for I am fearfully and wonderfully made; Marvelous are Your works, and that my soul knows very well."- Psalms 139:13-14

Prayer,

God this was hard. This brought up memories many of us have worked tirelessly to forget for decades. Lord, comfort us. Send your ministering angels to out sides right now. Please do not leave us uncovered. God touch those area of us right now that feel naked and ashamed.

Love on us Jesus. Bless us to know that our molestation was not our fault. A sick sexual predator took advantage of our innocence. We could not have provoked that.

It is not our job to defend the actions of our abusers. It is our responsibility to forgive them. Lord please help us to do just that. We cannot forgive them without your help. Set us free from the trauma and pain of having been molested. Bless us to think, live, and love as if it never happened to us. These and all things we pray in the matchless and amazing name of Jesus, I pray, Amen.

Reflection Time

Write to God about how this story made you feel. Ask Him to spread out in your heart like a healing balm.

_____

_____

_____

_____

_____

_____

_____

_____

_____

_____

The following scriptures are some of my go to scriptures when reliving a difficult time, such as the above. Meditate on them.

"I would have lost heart, unless I had believed
That I would see the goodness of the Lord
In the land of the living."- Psalms 27:13

"You will keep *him* in perfect peace,

Whose mind *is* stayed *on You,"- Isaiah 26:3*

"Be anxious for nothing, but in everything by prayer and supplication, with thanksgiving, let your requests be made known to God; [7] *and the peace of God, which surpasses all understanding, will guard your hearts and minds through Christ Jesus."– Philippians 4:6-7*

Chapter Twenty-Five
High School Daze

"Oh, give thanks to the Lord, for He is good!
For His mercy endures forever."- Psalms 136:1

I was on a path to self- destruction. Heck, I even touched down there and suffered for a while. I was a wounded soul. I was not a "bad girl." I was screaming and no one on earth could pick up my frequency. I was sending signals, but no one detected them.

I continued to slip under the radar. Flying as a hidden figure into the darkness of danger, desperation, and depression.

I ran down my crazy roads— full speed. I ignored ALL warning signs, yield, and even stop signs. I was attracted to risks. I used to do stupid stuff in my tweens like stealing lip gloss, and graffiti. Hey, do not judge me. I thought I was being hard. I know I had nothing on the tweens these days. That is actually very sad.

I upped my game when I hit my teens. I had no sense of self-worth. I had no regard for my own body. I gave it away to a couple of knuckle head boys during the eighth grade. I had them on rotating schedules before Daddy got home from work. Molestation often opens the gate to promiscuity. Oh wait, I said High School Daze, right?

I began to experiment with alcohol here and there. Heck I worked as a Nurse's Aide at a local facility, and the older Aides would invite me to hang out with them by the time I was sixteen. They were like "Smoke this. Try this pill. Want a drink?"

I was sixteen and thinking, *"You are grown as h*** and know this is illegal. However, pass it on over here."* I would pray all the way home, *Sweet Jesus, please do not let Mama smell this on me.* Sometimes I came up with convincing lies...Sometimes.

Thank God, I never really liked it. I drank it just to be cool, or to be doing something. However, I was too much of a control freak to like being out of control.

Same thing with weed. I did like it a little better than alcohol though. However, that came with the late teens. My sons crack up like, "Ma, you used to smoke?" I have to laugh at myself, "Like yeah, it was on very rare occasions though."

You all would have to know how square I am to find the hilarity in this.

Anyway...

I kind of felt like my life did not matter. I continued to live a dual life. I was a, "good girl" as far as my parents were concerned. I stayed on the honor roll. I did not get in much trouble at home, well other than missing curfew, and being a little too mouthy.

I would not have missed curfew if it were not for them darn boys to men. Like, I literally loved everything from older teenaged boys to young men, depending on how old I was as a teenager.

All I can say is God loves me for real. I was so hardheaded. I cannot even sit here and say I did everything because of the horrible things that happened to me. Did they shape my trajectory? Sure. However, some of the choices I made, was me being Twila.

It is *surely* because of His grace and mercy that I am still here today. All the stuff I have done, he could have snuffed my life out at any moment, but he kept giving me chance after chance. That is love.

God, I thank You for your undying love, grace, and mercy towards me.

Reflection Time

What are you doing *because you want to,* but blaming on your childhood? Ask God to help you to **stop it.** It is stripping you of your Self-Worth.

_____

_____

_____

_____

_____

_____

_____

_____

_____

_____

_____

_____

_____

_____

"Create in me a clean heart, O God,
And renew a steadfast spirit within me."- Psalms 51:10

Prayer

God, we love you. Thank you for loving us unconditionally. There is no other love like yours. God, I have blamed so many of my addictions, sins, and faulty thoughts on what my father did, what this person, or that person did, when in reality I made the choice. I ask for your forgiveness now.

Lord please pluck out everything in me that blinds me from my own ways. I love you with all my heart and do not desire to sin against you. The truth is, the heart that I love you from, is not pure.

Please Lord, create in me a clean heart, and renew a right spirit within me.

I love you God. Thank You for being patient with me.

Amen

Still Here by God's Grace

"Surely goodness and mercy shall follow me
All the days of my life;" Psalms 23: 6

Chapter Twenty-Six
I'm Going Down

By the time I was seventeen, my parents argued all the time. It started when I was twelve. Every other argument they were getting a divorce. Every other weekend my nerves were shot.

I was slow to learn back then. Why I did not pick up the pattern and realize nobody was leaving? I am just not sure. Mind boggling. I got upset each time. This is hilarious now. It was miserable then. Their drama really was enough to drive me to drinking.

I was the queen of escapism. I could travel miles away in my mind whether I was alone, when hanging with my Christopher, or with my girls.

I made my life as fun as possible. I spent time away from home a lot. It was getting closer to graduation time, and I was finally starting to come out of my shell.

I had met my best friends Kim, Sherry, Mary, and Vikki. We talked and hung out from time to time. I also spent time with my friend Kraig.

Oh my goodness, we had so much fun together. I was a giggle box. I think it was during these years, I discovered my comedy streak. I learned to laugh away my pain.

I would drink from time to time. I never really liked alcohol very much. My crack was boys at this point, more specifically, sex. Drinking and driving was not thought to me. I even let boys I barely knew, drive my brand- new Camaro. Seriously? SERIOUSLY.

More important than that pretty red metal, was ME. I just could not see. My God, I just had no clue about self - love, worth, or preservation.

My world was so chaotic, and I was spiraling out of control. I thank God for keeping His hands on me. I would truly have lost my mind or ended my life if He had not held me together. He was my glue-like for real.

Chapter Twenty-Seven
Black Out

"For He shall give His angels charge over you,
To keep you in all your ways"- Psalms 91:11

One Sunny day in April of 1985, I decided to hang out with Yvette. We maintained our friendship over the years. We had a few things in common.

.

Yvette had this idea for me to ride with her to meet one of her boyfriend's friends at Residence Park that day.

The hairs all stood up on the back of my neck at her mention of this. I had the most uneasy feeling. Not wanting to disappoint people, against all better judgement, I agreed to go.

Everything within me, screamed, *"DON'T GO!"*

I did not realize this was my discernment in overdrive that bright sunny day.

Against my better judgement, I hooked up with her to meet up with two guys she knew. I knew Christopher, the love of my life, would not approve. Heck my spirit did not approve *at all*.

I chucked caution to the wind and said let's do it. I was always the Dare Devil, or whatever it is called.

Mind you, this was just two days before my Debutante Ball.

Yvette's friend picked us up from her house. He told me he had a friend up at Residence Park that he wanted me to meet.

Something did not feel right about this whole set up. I started to back out. I really did. Afraid of disappointing man, I put myself at risk.

My God, I wish I would have just said no, and went back home. I started feeling so anxious on the inside. I had no idea why. I went for a ride that changed my life.

We arrived at the park and her friend introduced me to his friend "Goose." I am thinking "Goose" is old as heck. I surveyed the park. I had an Aunt Dot that lived within walking distance, and my Aunt Elaine.

My discernment said to walk away, and just go to one of their homes. It is as if the Holy Spirit was saying, "Daughter run- JUST RUN!"

You know how Spike Lee does that slow-motion effect in his movies when something is about to go down?

That is exactly how things seemed for me.

Everything my mother and father had taught me, I laid to the wayside. It was drilled into my head from the time I was at least thirteen to never lay your drinks down and walk away. Shoot for this matter, "don't talk to strangers" would have been effective.

This friend of Yvette's friend, Goose was his name offered me a cup of Rum and Coke, that he had premade. I looked at the cup, at his hand, at his grin. Then slowly, I drank from the devil's cup. And just then...

Everything went black...pitch black.

Chapter Twenty-Eight
I Just Wanted My Mama

"Hope deferred makes the heart sick" -Proverbs 13:12

I floated in and out of consciousness, although I stayed mostly out. When I could, all I could think was, *take me to my Mama girl. Yvette...Yvette*

My eyes flittered open as I fought to come back to consciousness. We were in a car...I was sitting in the front seat. Yvette's boyfriend was trying to put my hand on his crouch. This was not good.

I could remember us driving past a grocery store on Western Avenue, you know right where it intersects with Rosedale Drive?

I kept telling myself to stay awake, because I was almost home...to my Mama.

Hours later I woke up being raped. Apparently, he had raped me repeatedly. I made out my surroundings and realized I was directly across the street from my house.

Please take me to my Mama. Please. I do not think these words ever escaped my mouth because he looked at me like a sex crazed lunatic, and continued to force himself upon me.

I had no strength to fight him. I blacked out again…

Chapter Twenty-Nine
Please Just Take Me Home

"God is our refuge and strength,
A very present help in trouble."- Psalms 46:1

I finally came two enough to demand Goose to STOP!
Prior to this, I thought I was telling him to stop. I was
crying this out in the midst of fighting for consciousness.
The words never parted my lips though, I guess. I must
have been too drugged to speak them. He was an adult. I
was a teen. I was overpowered. Truthfully, he probably
was tired after Lord only knows how many rounds of
having his way with me. I had no concept of time. I just
knew I saw glimpses of light when we arrived back on
Rosedale Drive.

By the time I staggered to try to find my clothes, and
make my way, alone, and disoriented, it was almost
pitch-black outside.

At any rate, I was able to stagger and find my clothes.
I remember later discovering that I had put my panties on
inside out, in my hurry to escape. This would be my
painful confirmation that what I hoped did not happen,
really did.

I managed to ask Yvette how she could dare let this happen to me. She said, "I thought you were having fun." I remember asking her, "How when I was not even conscious?"

She did not even walk me across the street to my mother. I had to fend for myself. This is the same girl that I befriended out of sympathy when I was nine, who had the father with the wandering hands.

Some friendships just proved to be too costly.

Dazed, confused, and weak, I stumbled up the street. I fell into a good friend named Rodney who just happened to be visiting his uncle at the time.

Rodney hugged me as I struggled to tell him what just happened to me. He held me with so much care.

He gingerly walked me across the street to my mother.

I knew her healing hugs would make everything alright.

Rodney, I am forever grateful that God placed you in the right place at the right time. You were the angel I needed my friend.

SURELY, God was on my side. There is no telling where I would have ended up that night. I thank and praise God from the depths of my soul for sparing my life!

I could not have defended my airway, or anything else that day.

Reflection Time

This was heavy. Talk to God. He is our healer and comforter.

"Do not let your heart be troubled (afraid, cowardly). Believe [confidently] in God and trust in Him, [have faith, hold on to it, rely on it, keep going and] believe also in Me."- John 14:1

_____

_____

_____

_____

_____

_____

_____

_____

_____

_____

_____

_____

God please heal us everywhere we hurt. Please mend our broken hearts as only you can. We love you God and say thank You. In Jesus' name, Amen.

This was the most difficult chapter to write. I cried and cried, even to edit this, I weep. This baby girl was never consoled. Her tears, her sobs, her bleeding all blended in with the yelling and screaming of arguing parents in the background.

She went on to make her parents proud, and performed well at the Debutante ball, all while being utterly crushed on the inside. Who would hold her together as she fell apart? Who could hold the pieces of Twila's broken heart?

"The Lord is near to the brokenhearted,
and saves the crushed in spirit". - Ps. 34:18 NRSV

Writing this made me realize I had not faced the pain and unforgiveness I felt about Yvette leaving me hanging that day. Yvette, I forgive you. We have never really talked about that day. Yet, I love you and I forgive you.

For decades, I had blocked being raped completely out. I had it tucked way down in some level of unconsciousness. While writing, I literally, experienced the pain and sickness of it as I typed this for you. I have to release the pain in order to experience the fullness of God's healing.

For those like me that have been violated, I am sincerely sorry that you experienced this type of violation in your life. YOU DID NOT DESERVE IT.

Today, I VALIDATE YOUR ABUSE. Today, I pray that you feel the loving arms of God wrapped around you, in the most loving and comforting of ways.

I pray that you can trust HIS touch. I know many of us have "touch issues." This HEAVENLY FATHER will never harm us, molest us, or mishandle us.

What is comforting is knowing that WE ARE NOT ALONE. GOD DOES NOT LEAVE US. God didn't walk out on us then, and He won't abandon us during the process of our healing, or any other time for that matter. He is ever-present with us.

His Promises are true. "I will never leave nor forsake you." Hebrews 11:5." "God is our refuge and strength, A very *present* help in trouble." -Psalms 46:1

God, we are tired, it has been draining trying to cover up this pain for so long. Can you heal us for real? I mean for real. We are tired of getting temporary breakthroughs on Sunday mornings, only to be triggered by Tuesday and drug back down to the familiar place of sadness and heaviness,

Lord please make us to be free indeed. We are no longer in the abusive places, thank you for this. Please take the abusive places out of us. It is like you freeing the people out of Egypt but them having an Egyptian mentality still.

Deliver us oh God, from a victim mentality Lord. Show us how to think, dream, breathe, feel, hope, walk, talk, and truly live victoriously oh Lord. Restore our worth Lord. Help us to see ourselves as fearfully and wonderfully made, and as marvelous works.

It is in your perfect name I pray, Amen.

Chapter Thirty

I Thought You Loved Me God. This one hurt. By now, I had developed more of a relationship with God. I went to church more. I understood God to be a protector. It was my understanding that God could do anything.

As a seventeen-year-old believer, I wanted to know why the God of Heaven and Earth did not protect His daughter from being raped.

I wanted to know WHY?

I had been disappointed by my father, my unreliable friend," and now it seemed as though God turned His back on me too.

Did life get better than this? Is there a reason to live? I literally ask God at times, "How did You let this happen?"

I do not know about you all, but I have asked God this on many occasions. He rarely, if ever answers me. He is not obligated to. It just hurts my heart to know that an all-powerful God could have stopped my molestation and rape, but did not.

You can give me scripture all day long. He just did not. He could have stopped my loved ones from dying, but did not, you follow me? This list could go on.

I believe if you are honest with yourselves, you have had some of the same conversations with God as well.

I did much soul searching. I basically had to decide to either trust God, or not. Thankfully, I made the right choice. I felt like Job must have felt. I grabbed hold of the yet in my spirit. *"Though He slay me, yet will I trust Him." – Job 13:15*

I have cried out to God in desperate need of understanding of how an ALLPOWERFUL GOD, does not STOP tragedy before it happens. How is that an OMNIPRESENT, OMNIPOTENT. OMNISCIENT GOD, does he not protect his innocent boys and girls, men and women?

The truth that GOD allowed this to happen, makes me cry today. YET, I trust God. YET, I forgive God. Yes, forgive God. I was angry with him, for allowing harm to come my way, when I knew He had the capacity to stop it.

We really can release the heaviness of our molestation and trauma. We can be free from it all.

Give it over to God. This happened to you. It is not the definition of who you are.

The enemy set so many traps to not just hurt me, but to destroy me. Some of them I discerned, and some I did not. However, God is greater. His plans for my life shall come to pass.

My life took *many* detours, ditches, and dives. However, I am ever so grateful to still be alive. God is able. He has shown himself so strong in my life.

I am still standing. Guess what! So are you!

This is not by coincidence. This is by God's special design for you. God has a perfect plan for your life. He needs you to only believe.

If it had been up to me, I would have said deuces to life a long time ago. I was over it. Life for real. I did not want to hear another church song. I was tired of sermons with no power.

Sick of it. Then one day, God gave me the strength to hope again. He helped me to come up from the pit of despair.

I had grown accustomed to pit living, so the light was blinding at first. However, for every good day, and even the not so good days. I thank God above for not leaving me where I preferred to stay.

I was depressed, defeated, and despondent. I was just existing. Have you ever been here?

You know, you get up get dressed, go through the motions of living, without experiencing life. Yeah, that was me for a very long time.

I would have moments of peace, and even moments of happiness, only to be drawn back down into the all too familiar place of blah.

I was walking-dead.

I nodded at the appropriate times in conversations. I even had a smile. It just did not radiate from within. On the inside, though, I was screaming. "Help Me! Help Me Please God! I don't want to die, but I cannot go on living like this."

No one around me could perceive my scream. So, I SCREAMED…and SCREAMED and SCREAMED.

Just when I had given up hope of ever escaping the trap of misery my life had become, something happened.

The Pit Snatcher grabbed me out!

"He brought me up out of the pit of destruction, out of the miry clay, And He set my feet upon a rock making my footsteps firm."- Psalms 40:2 (NASB)

When I look back at the mess I dealt with, not to mention the messes I made, I have no choice but to be grateful to God. God is faithful!

So many times, if we never look back at our pasts, we want to convince everyone, including ourselves that we have arrived. By doing so, we cannot address the brokenness and jacked up patterns we have. If we don't look at our crazy, we can't fix our crazy.

I am not suggesting we go and pitch a tent to dwell in our pasts. I am suggesting, that we go back and examine what makes us tick.

Do some self -examination.

When you find yourself repeating the same patterns, relationship after relationship, job after job, church after church, then the problem just might be you.

Give it over to God. This happened to you. It is not the definition of who you are.

You are a survivor. You are triumphant over what tried to label, oppress, and keep you down.

To every man and woman, boy or girl, who is reading this book. There is hope for you after molestation.

You are beautiful. You may feel broken; however, you are beautifully broken. God blesses what he breaks. He uses what is broken for His glory.

We are never broken beyond repair.

Guess what? As we tell our stories of being harmed, molested, and mishandled, we get freed up from the shame of it. We also find that it begins to hurt a little less.

We don't have to walk around with our heads bowed down. We did not cause the abuse. We did not entice our molesters or rapists

God catapult us into our purposes in You. God is sure to perform through us, what he created us for. He is faithful to perform it. As I look back over my trauma, it really does make sense that I am drawn to encouraging hurting women.

God really does take what the devil meant for evil, and use it for good. I am confident that so many people will be helped by the testimony and triumph of my story.

I can relate to women on such an amazing level when I minister, because I am not fake about what I have endured. I am a survivor, who has not forgotten what I survived. Most importantly, I have not forgotten the God that brought me out!

If it had not been for the Lord on my side, I have no idea where I would be, or if I would even be alive!

It is God who orders our steps. He is going to do everything He said He was going to do, for us, to us, and through us. He is infallible. He is God.

Chin up, you did not miss your chance to shine. Don't focus on the time wasted. Focus on lessons learned.

"For I am confident of this very thing, that He who began a good work in you will perfect it until the day of Christ Jesus."- Philippians 1:6 NASB

Truthfully, I had to become confident in my confession. It took many years before I felt confident about the good work god was doing through me— with me.

I have really entered the rest and assurance of this promise within this past year. I am telling you, I have been on this amazing fast track of faith during my writing journey. It has been unbelievable.

Chapter Thirty-One
Forgiveness

"In prayer there is a connection between what God does and what you do. You can't get forgiveness from God, for instance, without also forgiving others. If you refuse to do your part, you cut yourself off from God's part." – Matthew 6: 14-15 MSG

Merriam Webster defines the word forgive as the following:

-to stop feeling anger toward (someone who has done something wrong): to stop blaming (someone)
: to stop feeling anger about (something): to forgive for (something wrong): to stop requiring payment of (money that is owed)

Listen here, this definition gave me my entire life! This is the key to freedom for you all. My God! It is spelled out right there before us.

This is where spirit meets practical! God tells us that we must forgive to be forgiven. How can God forgive us if we have anger and vengefulness built up in our hearts towards another?

Can you see this?

Jesus! To stop feeling anger towards another, does not make them right, it makes us right with God. We do not have to worry about whether or not they will "get what's coming to them."

Yeah, I know that phrase all too well. That mindset held me up from freedom for far too long. Man listen, do not worry about them. They are not thinking about you. Be concerned about yourself, getting free, being free, and staying free is a full-time job for me.

I do not know about you all. However, I simply do not have enough time in my day to be concerned about who hurt me and whether or not they got theirs.

"Vengeance is mine says the Lord, I will repay." (Romans 12:19)

I looked at the scriptural reference for this passage, and was just like wow God.

"Vengeance is Mine, and recompense;
Their foot shall slip in due time; "Deuteronomy 32:35

My motto now is *"God can pay them back, much better than I ever could."* I will let God deal with them.

This is not always my initial response. A sister's flesh will rise up. However eventually, my Helper, the Holy Spirit leads me back to this attitude.

This Word of God matches up with the third leg of the definition of forgive- "to stop requiring payment." My God, as I said before, spirit lines up with natural.

Forgiveness therefore is the act of forgiving. I used to erroneously think holding on to unforgiveness gave me power over the person that wronged me. What I found out, was that the opposite was true.

The longer I refused to forgive someone for the offense against me, the more consumed I became with the them, and their actions.

The more consumed with them I became, the more time I thought about them, obsessed over them and paying them back.

Before I knew it, my whole day and sometimes night, was consumed by the person I was upset with. I was light weight obsessed with them.

Who had the control? They had it. Unforgiveness is not a boss move at all. Forgiveness is. Forgiveness frees you up to move on.

Forgiveness freed me up. It has freed me up more during this writing process to be perfectly honest with you. God has shown me blind spots and pockets where I still harbored residue of unforgiveness for my poor deceased father for not validating me when I needed him.

I had to have a talk with myself like, "Girl if you do not let this man rest. He has been dead for twenty-one years. Let him rest in the name of Jesus."

It hurt me to know in my heart that I even had unforgiveness, Heck, I did not know I did. Without self - examination, dangerous emotions can grow inside of us like a cancer. It is imperative that we ask the Holy Spirit to strip search us from time to time and show us if we have something hidden in our cavities.

Bitterness kills. Grudges kill. They do not kill the people we hold the grudge against, they kill us. Whether this death, is spiritual, emotional, or physical, it is far too high a price to pay.

Now I will be transparent with you, this part of forgiveness has always been the hardest for me. I wanted to see the people that hurt me, hurt. I am just being real.

Now I did not want God to strike them down, well maybe one person, (that's another book though.) I did want God to prick their hearts in such a way that they could feel the pain and misery I was feeling— and I had felt.

However, when we ask God to show us how to *really* forgive from or hearts, we relinquish the need to see the other person suffer. We are satisfied with the apology we never receive.

For me, this was and is a process. Some people say they forgive instantly. I have not been that saint. I just have not.

I have said the words, "I forgive you," to people that hurt me. I would pray with faith too, and believe in my heart, that I had forgiven them.

Then I would notice my body tensing up whenever I saw them and be pissed off. I mean livid. I would see them smile and be happy, and my attitude would be jacked up for the rest of the day.

But my confession was I forgave them? Yeah right.

My talk was not matching my walk at all. God had more work to do on me.

Chapter Thirty-Two
A Spirit of Forgiveness

I had to come to the realization that I needed to learn how to forgive. I cried out, *"God show me how to forgive with every fiber of my being. God show me how to forgive from my heart, and not just my lips. Help me to forgive others like you forgave me.*

Lord, deliver me from the need to see other's pay for what they have done to me. Jesus help me!

God, I am so angry. I don't want to be like this. I cannot go on living like this. I cannot teach and preach to others to be loving and forgiving, yet be so unforgiving. God help me! Remove every muscle memory attached to the offense that makes my body respond to their presence. God please give me a Spirit of Forgiveness.

In the name of Jesus, I pray,
Amen."

God answered my prayer! It was through his Spirit, that I could truly forgive people that had hurt me, and forgive myself, in order to move forward.

I encourage you to do the same.

If you say you have forgiven someone, yet you stalk their Facebook page, spend your days and nights obsessing over them and/or who they are in a relationship with now, you have not forgiven them.

Seek God for help now. Your soul, sanity, and peace of mind depends on it. Get yourself together.

During this writing process, God showed me places where I harbored unforgiveness for others. I had to cry out to the Father for Help. I thought I had forgiven them a long time ago. Yet unforgiveness had found a pocket inside of my heart and resided there for years.

God had to open me up to reveal it, and remove it. I am so glad he did. While he was in there operating on me, he showed me there was a second pocket of infection in my heart that was trying to kill me. It was called unforgiveness of myself.

I prayed, and cried because I thought I loved myself better than that now. I thought I had forgiven myself of everything *by now.*

I was faced with a decision. Hang out in denial, or deal with the discovery. I said God snatch that infectious hinderance out! I have too much life to live!

I was created to fly like a beautiful bird. But my unforgiveness was holding my wings down.

Chapter Thirty-Three
Forgiveness Empowers Us to Move Forward

Please pray for God to show you how to forgive. I have spent much of my life holding on to the pain of my abuse. It did happen. It was horrible. Nothing takes away from that. Forgiveness has taught me to say, "Ok God, I trust you to handle the perpetrator."

When we forgive those that hurt us, we no longer remain paralyzed by our anger, and fear. We no longer spend endless hours thinking about the person, or persons that did us dirty.

In this way, our power and energy is given back to us, instead of wasted on the perpetrator.

Forgiveness unlocks you from the prison bars of your misery. For so long, I handed my strength back to a past that could not help me walk forward.

Forgiving the person that hurt us, never makes them right. It just frees us from being wrong for not forgiving them.

Unforgiveness is a bitter poison that keeps your mind running, like a gerbil on an exercise wheel thinking, "If only I would have, should have, or could have..." I have done this for far too long. Step off the wheel.

I am determined to spend the rest of my days living forward. I want all the blessings God has for me and my life. I cannot get them if I am facing yesterday.

What about you? Are you ready for your NOW blessings?

Help someone by telling them what God has brought you through. I pray my writing is helping you.

Reflection Time:

Take time and pray. Ask God to show you who you need to forgive. Use the space below to journal what the Holy Spirit reveals to you.

Chapter Thirty-Four
Examine Your Self Talk

"And, behold, a woman, which was diseased with an issue of blood twelve years, came behind him, and touched the hem of his garment:

For she said within herself, If I may but touch his garment, I shall be whole.

But Jesus turned him about, and when he saw her, he said, Daughter, be of good comfort; thy faith hath made thee whole. And the woman was made whole from that hour."- Matthew 9: 20-21

Hype Yourself Up

We need to be our own hype person, like the Woman with the Issue of Blood was. She did not need a hype man. She encouraged herself, right on to the place of her breakthrough.

She is absolutely my favorite woman in the Bible. Like me, she had been going through her ordeal for a minute. Like me, she did not appear to have much of a support group. Also, much like me, she stayed in her head a lot.

She was sick and tired of being sick and tired. Has anybody ever been there? She had been to doctor after doctor, for them to experiment on her and still not help her. Now that her money was funny, she got word that, Jesus was coming through that day. OMG!

Hurting, tired, bleeding, weak, but full of faith and curiosity, she pressed her way. She was desperate. She did not care what all those stuck up church women were going to say about her this time, she was going for hers.

She did not have time, to wait for the church announcements to be read. She did not care whether this was the fast song or slow song, or whether Jesus was about to preach the Word. She took a deep breath, went down low, and reached for her healing. Jesus was touched.

Not only had she touched His hem, but this woman touched Jesus' heart. She was not trying to cause a scene. She was trying to slip away unnoticed. Jesus knew her story, without her even telling Him. He was familiar with the customs of the culture.

More than that, the Savior knew what this woman with faith, stood in need of. He called her to Himself. She wanted her body healed. She received that immediately. Jesus called her Daughter and restored her Soul. This woman had been a reject and had not known her worth for twelve whole years. She was kicked out, and disregarded. Jesus let her know, that she was a part of the Kingdom of God! He healed her hemorrhaging heart as well. He touched her in a way she had never been touched before. It all started with a thought. What are you saying to yourselves?

Arise Woman You Have Worth!

This Woman is Savage! I am going to be just like Her! I have alluded to her, let me just stop and post her story here.

Her story is so amazing, her faith so profound, she gets mentioned in all three of the Synoptic Gospels. Matthew, Mark, and Luke. This Sister is bad you all!

I am not here to do an exegesis of this text. I just want to stop by here to tell you, there is power in your press! Keep reaching, keep pressing, keep believing! You have come too far to give up now. Don't you *dare* go back home, bleeding and stinking. Healing is the children's bread.

My God, she had been shunned from society. This woman had forgotten what it felt like to be loved and connected to anyone. Here *JESUS* you all, calls her *DAUGHTER!* WHAT?! Wait, daughter?! I know she looked around like, is He talking to me? Me. the one that no one wanted to fool with for twelve years?

Listen, I do not know about you all, but the fact that Jesus, the Son of the Living God, calls me Daughter, negates all the negative things that any one has ever said about me.

In an instant, one word from God, can make everything alright. One touch. -Daughter.

Not only does she receive healing for her body. She receives healing for her lonely and rejected soul. Her worth was restored! I submit to you, not only did she stop hemorrhaging from her womb, but she also, instantaneously stopped hemorrhaging from her heart.

What she received on that day, was her worth.

She heard in the spirit, "Daughter You have Worth!"

Consider the Woman, with the Issue of Blood. My God. She tried everything her intellect suggested to her. She spent all her resources in an effort to be healed.

She was not passive about her healing, at all. She did not sit on the outskirts of society and bleed to death. She surely could have. Society, in her context, told her she was damaged.

She was an outcast. It is not like her squad was encouraging her and believing God was with her for a miracle. This did not stop her though.

She was relentlessly in pursuit of her breakthrough. God showed me, I must be the same way. She did not deny the fact that she had issues.

Many of us miss our opportunities to be delivered from bondage and sickness, because we won't be honest enough with ourselves to acknowledge that, WE NEED GOD.

The Woman with the Issue of Blood, PRESSED HER WAY to her breakthrough! Let me encourage you today, GET UP!

It is no longer about what "they" said about you? What are you saying about you? Most importantly, what does God say about you?

"For she said within herself, If I may but touch his garment, I shall be whole." – Matthew 9:21 KJV

God showed me that I had to change my self -talk. Victory is available to me. However, I had to stop talking myself out of it, before I went for it.

I also had to stop describing myself by what I suffered, and describe myself by what I survived. I had to change my name from victim, to victor! I now describe myself in positive terms and life-giving words. I love how, when God changed names in the Bible, he changed the people to reflect their destiny. (ex. Saul-Paul, Abram-Abraham.)

God speaks victory and destiny into us today. He calls us more than conquerors. God knows who we are. It is necessary for us to petition God, with forward facing lenses, so we can speak life into now and out tomorrows.

We may have been hurt, abused, and mistreated before. There may be people in our lives now, who are crazy enough to put their mouths on God's anointed ones.

Guess what? IT DOES NOT MATTER!

We will take our cues from God, and not man, about our merit. He said, we are more precious than rubies!

We may have felt valueless before, however, WE ARE WOMEN OF WORTH!

There is no stopping us now! We shall walk in our worth and see God's best for our lives! We will enjoy our own company, before we settle for frogs again.

Amen, somebody?

We are the most amazing people on the planet! God thinks so, and so should we!

We are more than conquerors!

We are overcomers!

We are show stoppers!

We don't need your applause, we will clap for ourselves!

We don't need your praise; our children and husbands shall call us blessed.

For the brothers reading this, you are a royal priesthood, a chosen generation. You do not need a woman to validate you. Believe what God says about you! Cook your own meals, buy your own gifts, iron your own clothes, before you settle for *anything less than a* Virtuous Wife.

You all, we made it through! God loves us too much for us to live a defeated life. If he wanted us to be stuck in our pasts, don't you know, He would have left us there?

You better live, while you have a chance. I know I am.

God Bless You!

We are Virtuous Women! You are Valuable Men. We will not settle for anything less than God's best, in and for our lives, ever again.

If I must dine alone until God sends my blessing, so be it. I am good company. I'll be darned, if I waste my time with another frog man. Look, they just will not turn into a prince, I do not care how much you lay hands on them suckers. (smile.)

Besides, all this goodness wrapped up in the complete package called T, needs a real King, sent by God.

I KNOW MY WORTH AND I AM WORTH THE WAIT!

There is still time for us to get our entire lives. My sisters and brothers, ARISE!

Tell yourself who you are. You are the Daughter, not just of any king, but THE KING. What? You are a bad sister! You must affirm yourself daily.

Sisters, we have to do better about telling ourselves who we are and *Whose* we are. If we do so, we won't think every scripture quoting devil is being prophetic. We can say, "Oh. I already know that, and actually you quoted that wrong."

Here are 5 Practical Tips to Build Your Self-Talk Game Up:

1. Read God's Word Daily
2. Pray God's Word Back to Him
3. Believe What God Says About You in His Word
4. Speak God's Word Over Your Life
5. Apply God's Word to Your Life

6.

What you say to yourself, makes the difference between getting delivered, or staying stuck. We saw that with the woman with the Issue of Blood.

She said, *"Man look, I am not about to sit here bleeding one more day. I bet I get healed today."*- Twila's Version

Reflection Time

What thought patterns are holding you back? Ask God to deliver you from them now, in the name of Jesus?

_____

_____

_____

_____

_____

_____

_____

_____

_____

_____

_____

God please heal our perspectives of self. Bless us to see ourselves through Your eyes. In the name of Jesus, I pray, Amen.

We must be candid and admit that we attracted a lot of negativity to ourselves because we did not think better of ourselves.

We believed the lies told to us by our own disturbed self-images, our past lovers or ex-spouses, our relatives who were verbally, sexually, and/or physically abusive, and anyone else that were caustic to our spirits.

God can deliver us from these mindsets, memories, and strongholds. He is mighty to deliver. We must fight for our freedom from low self -esteem with the same amount of fervor, if not more, as we would for our physical health.

If the devil can keep us down in our minds, he can keep us miserable. Fight for your peace. Peace doesn't come easily. We are told to seek it and pursue it.

However, the fact that we are told to seek peace, clues us in that it is possible to obtain. This is encouraging.

We are not alone in this battle. God is fighting for us. In fact, the victory already belongs to us. We must show up with our faith. We must do our part.

God had to put me in time out, not because of bad behavior per se. I was receiving Worth Lessons from Him. He taught me to love myself unconditionally.

God showed me how to embrace my past and present, and to accept that it is all working together for the good.

This has been a time of refreshing and renewal.

I had defective and destructive thought patterns and behaviors. I had to take ownership of my issues and reach out for the Hem of Jesus' garment, to be made whole.

I said within myself, If I can but touch the Hem of His garment, I will be made whole. I had learned by now, that healing was not enough. I needed a complete overhaul. I needed Jesus to make me whole.

I was relieved to find out that the length of illness was not a disqualifier for restoration. I had bled for a long time. I thought I could out run my pain.

I shopped, ate, and shopped some more. I laughed and chatted and put on a happy face. All the while, I wanted someone to reach and just hold this painful place in my heart.

THE LORD is teaching me that my stock is good, my voice is beautiful, my wings do soar, and my mind is great. My wealth is endless, my possibilities are limitless, my anointing is unquestionable, and my gifting is for sure.

GOD IS schooling me on my poetic-flow, my confident-stroll, and the ability to know, who is real and who is fake.

Baby Listen, the way my intrinsic value is set up in Christ, I am UNSTOPPABLE. SO ARE YOU! Women of Worth ARISE! GIRL GET UP, WITH YOUR BAD SELF!

Chapter Thirty-Five
Be Real to Get Healed

"and you will know the truth, and the truth will make you free."-John 8:32

Being honest about our pain, is the first step to receiving the help we need. I remember Rev. Lela Crawford once giving the example of going to the doctor's office for a sore bottom, but only revealing a hangnail when the doctor came in.

What do you think the doctor treated? The hangnail. That brother or sister walked up out of there, with the same pain in the behind they had when they walked up in there. Why? Because, they would not show they butt. This is probably the only scenario, when it is okay to show your behind.

Listen, you have to show God where it hurts. In the natural, the doctor cannot heal what he or she cannot see. In the spiritual, the DOCTOR often *will not* heal what we are not willing to reveal.

It is not that God is blind to it. We are. He wants us to catch the vision.

Beloved, we cannot live a truly free life if we never face our truths. Denial will wear us out. I have been that sister that tried to outrun her truth, on so many facets. It does not work. Truth always catches up with you.

I was dog-tired. Wearing a mask, is not cute at all. It is not fun. It hinders us from healing. We cannot heal from what we won't uncover. The thing about wearing a mask, is we think we are blocking other's from getting in. We are also blocking ourselves from breaking out.

Bacteria and infection multiply in wounds that cannot get air. If allowed to fester, an infection can take your very life. You better let God see that thing and put some healing balm on it. Show Him wear it hurts!

If you have been molested or raped and have not received counseling, whether spiritual or psychological, I am encouraging you to do this for yourself today. You are worth it. You deserve to be made whole. It is never too late to receive the help you need.

God pressed it upon my heart to expose my molestation and rape to you all. These were very tragic events to relive. I needed to though. Before, I just buried my tragedies, and was forced to keep moving like nothing occurred.

This time, I was able to wail before God for the scared and unprotected little girl, that never healed within. I was able to cry the tears, that I sniffed back over all the years since then. For once in my life, I did not have to be strong, or grown, or anything else but God's beautifully broken daughter.

Chapter Thirty-Six
It is Okay to Be Vulnerable to God

"Let us therefore come boldly to the throne of grace, that we may obtain mercy and find grace to help in time of need." – Hebrews 4:16

You are no less healed, faithful, or Christian if you admit you have issues. You will have, just stepped out of denial and faced the truth.

The hardest thing to do, once we become saved, is to say, "I hurt," or "I am sick". We have become so super saved, that we think we float. Dude, keep it real.

I have been around people darn near coughing up lungs. If I know they are the spooky deep saints, just for kicks, I will ask them how they are doing, just to hear their response, "Oh, I am fine. I am blessed and highly …cough…cough…favored…gasp…cough…in the Lord…" Yeah, okay. Your coughing butt needs some air and prayer.

Can we talk? Just tell the truth. Keep it real with yourself and God, at least. If we cannot be honest with ourselves, we are in a bad way. I can only say this from experience.

Look, are you still reading this book like tsk, tsk, what a shame she went through all of that. Dude, if you do not pinch yourself and WAKE UP! God did NOT have me going through everything I went through to write this book, for you to just check my sentence structures.

Get a revelation from God. God wants to heal *you* too. Never, ever, believe that you have it all together.

God desires to take you from faith to faith, and from glory to glory.

In order to do that, you have to drop the façade, and invite Him into your brokenness. To not do so, is straight foolishness.

To read this book, with all this Word up in here, with all the prayer, sacrifice, and discipline that went into me writing it, and not even consider, that God would have a word for you, would be such a sad state of your heart.

God loves you. Submit to *Him.*

"Submit yourselves therefore to God. Resist the devil, and he will flee from you." – James 4:7 KJV

Just knowing that He has the power to heal me, is enough for me. Is it enough for you? Beloved, be healed today? You have been covering and cowering, too long.

You have been enslaved to your abusers, too long.

Many of you are still locked up in your minds over imaginary consequences, from molesters that are dead and gone. God says, Arise. It's okay now. You can live.

They died, you did not.

Chapter Thirty-Seven
She Came Out of Hiding

What if the Woman with the Issue of Blood stayed out in the outskirts of the town, pretending she had no issues? She was determined to get healed and had sense enough to worship Jesus. That is a whole new book.

"And a woman who had a hemorrhage for twelve years, and could not be healed by anyone, [44] came up behind Him and touched the fringe of His cloak, and immediately her hemorrhage stopped. And Jesus said, "Who is the one who touched Me?" And while they were all denying it, Peter said, "Master, the people are crowding and pressing in on You." But Jesus said, "Someone did touch Me, for I was aware that power had gone out of Me." When the woman saw that she had not escaped notice, she came trembling and fell down before Him, and declared in the presence of all the people the reason why she had touched Him, and how she had been immediately healed. And He said to her, "Daughter,

your faith has made you well; go in peace." Luke 8:43-48
NASB

Where is *your* faith? Do you have crawling through the crowd of faith? This is my girl! She is savage!

This woman just needs a touch from Jesus. She is unlike many of us who would want a special title, front row seat, 10 letters attached to our Facebook names after an encounter. She just wanted her bleeding to stop.

Have you ever been so broken by people you thought you could trust, but they walked out on you? I want to know, am I the only one who has hemorrhaged to the point of not being able to change my own pad, wipe my own legs, or care if I smelled?

MY GOD MAKE THIS BLEEDING END!

She did not care…When you get to this place of suffering, you will run to Jesus, walk to Jesus, crawl to Jesus, you will make sure you get there.

Again, I ask you, how badly do you want to be made whole? In other words, how bad do you want it?

Reflection Time

Talk to God

_____

_____

_____

_____

_____

_____

_____

_____

_____

_____

_____

God, we need to hear you call us Daughter and Make Us Whole. Amen

Help is Available

As we heal, it may require spiritual, medical, and psychological components. This is okay.

God heals through His anointed vessels. Often times, that will include health professionals as well as His ministers (servants.)

You can talk to your Family Doctor or Primary Care Physician about your trauma. If you have no health insurance, there are Free Clinics everywhere. Most of them have an on-site Licensed Social Worker, that can offer you counseling.

If this is the case, speak to her/him about helping you apply for Medicaid, or whatever insurance would be appropriate for your financial and social situation. Everyone reading the words on this page, have the right to care.

I had to take responsibility for seeking help. I had to get over those who did not help me and praise God for giving me the resources to seek counseling for myself.

Look I had to tell myself, it is time out from blaming my deceased parents for not getting me help after my molestation and rape. I AM BLESSED TO work a good job, with plenty of benefits.

If I am in need of help now, there is NOTHING to keep me from getting it. The jig is up. Twila, quit blaming people for your issues. Get yourself together.

Physician, heal thyself. (Luke 4:23)

Your body sadly breaks down after many years and often decades, of living in a perpetual state of fight or flight. Stress hormones begin to attack not only your brain, but also every living cell in your body. Beloved, get yourself some help.

Talking to someone, other than your pastor, *if you need to,* is okay. That is your right. That is your business. If your pastor's ego is so fragile that he or she can't handle you getting help outside of their house of worship, you are clearly in the wrong house.

Get yourself some help. With all the help available in this age, there really is no excuse for not getting assistance with your issues. We have the capacity to heal.

There are no hopeless cases. We serve the God of hope. Ask Him for direction. We shall be made whole, IF we reach for the Hem of Jesus' garment.

Please seek assistance for your children if they begin to exhibit changes in their behavior. The change in their behavior, is often a symptom of a deeper issue they cannot explain.

Children, by nature, love to please their parents. Sudden changes in their disposition or behavior patterns, can be an indication that the child is experiencing internal distress. Make an appointment with your child's primary care physician. Then, take it from there.

Take the time, to get the proper help. It can save your life. It can change the future of your baby's life.

We know what it is like to suffer in silence. Let's be there for our children.

I missed a LOT of stuff in my children. That is why I can write with so much passion. When you know better, do better. I want you to be better than me. Heck, each day, I am better than I was the day before.

You are OBLIGATED to get that child some help.

This may or may not be an indication that something deeper is going on.

Do not let this go unchecked. If you do, you may allow them to slip into deep psychological illnesses, or even suicide. Please ask the questions.

It is not my intention to make you hurt. I want you to confront your issues, realize you need the Savior to heal, and petition Him to be made free indeed. This may have stirred up bad memories or triggers for you.

Reflection Time

Take the time now, to write out how you are feeling. Pray for God to heal you in the areas of your blind spots. *Leave no area open that needs to be sealed Lord.* Ask God to heal you and make you whole in the name of Jesus, it is so.

_____

_____

_____

_____

_____

_____

_____

_____

_____

_____

_____

Chapter Thirty-Eight
Get Yourself Together!

Kayla started having temper tantrums when she was like nine months old. Bump waiting for terrible two's, this baby girl would wild out. Her temper would go from 0-100 in a matter of seconds.

You know I was laying hands and casting out the spirit of anger, right? She did not know. She thought MiMi was just putting oil on her little forehead (smile).

I knew Little Mama's temperament, well enough to know her cues. When I saw her tension building, I would divert her attention to try to prevent her from experiencing a complete meltdown. After all, who wants to feel all out of sorts? It is exhausting.

I realized, if I could create a pattern of self-soothing in Kayla, or recognize her distress early on, whether it be a furrowed brow, a back arch, her pulling on her ear, her grunting in frustration, or her beginning to fuss, I could help her not to escalate.

You all will not believe what worked. I would gain eye to eye contact with my lovebug (shift her focus), change my voice (shift her atmosphere), and command her to "*Get yourself together*!" Kayla would burst out in the cutest giggles ever!

We have heard it said, that hurting people hurt people. This is true. That will only fly but for so long. You cannot use this as an excuse to stay stuck in dysfunction. It is time to rise up and GET YOURSELF TOGETHER!

Chapter Thirty-Nine
A New Heart

I remember going to see my primary physician about twelve years ago. She read my list of ailments. There were at least seven on there. She went down and checked off each ailment and said, "stress related, stress related..."

Some of the stress was from external stressors going on in my life. I am certain that the majority of my stress, was coming from the disharmony and unrest I had within.

I wanted to say a quick prayer, recite a scripture, and call myself healed. God required me to bare my heart to Him, so that he could remove the stony places.

I will give you a new heart and put a new spirit within you; I will take the heart of stone out of your flesh and give you a heart of flesh. -Ezekiel 36:26

I had to trust Him to remove the callouses. They were just tough places with decreased *blood* flow.

God needed to do a spiritual coronary artery bypass graft. The surgeon needed to reattach my blocked vessels to a new heart, so the Blood of Jesus could flow effectively through me, to give me my life back.

You and I will live life abundantly, without the fear of man. Jesus came, so that we can do just that. It is the devil that wants us worn, depressed, and suffering. He wants to steal our joy, peace, and hope.

I don't know about you, but I am going to be about living the abundant life for the rest of my days. I want what Jesus wants for me. I have learned that I do not aim high enough with my desires.

I give God this wimpy prayer list like, Lord please make my life good, Amen.

He is like, "Good? Wait do you know who I am? I am the Great I AM! Why would I stop at giving you a good life, when I have already paved the way for you to have so much better?"

I blocked that rape completely out. I had it tucked down deeply in my heart.

I literally, experienced the pain and sickness of it, as I typed this for you. I have to release the pain, in order to experience the fullness of God's healing.

On Sunday October 8th, 2017, I confronted all of the details of my rape, and forgave my rapist.

There was one person, I needed to forgive. I had to forgive my mother for not being there for me or taking me to get therapy.

She shared with me, things that had almost happened to her as she grew up... I am thinking, that is just how things were dealt with in her generation and the generations before us.

It was a common occurrence. You simply cried, cleaned yourself up, and kept it moving. Of course, there is nothing simple about such a complex issue.

So, I wept.

Prayer

God, we have dealt with so much as children. We cry over things that happened decades ago because it still hurts us. Please Lord, release us from the pain of yesterday so we can enjoy today. Bless us with the spirit of forgiveness. Show us how to forgive those who knowingly, or unknowingly hurt us or our loved ones.

Give us peace over our pasts. Help us to let go. Bless us with freedom to enjoy our present situations. Bless us God, with new loves, memories, and opportunities. Help us to rejoice in our "now".

Lord, we have been prisoner to our pasts, too long. Set us free in the name of Jesus, I pray. Amen!

Chapter Forty
Knowing My Worth

"Who can find a virtuous woman? for her price is far above rubies."- Proverbs 31:10 KJV

I spent so much of my life not knowing my worth. I thought my actions defined me. I believed my worth was stolen from me when I was molested as a girl, then raped as a teen.

I was blind to my inner beauty and value. I was ignorant to my wealth, royalty, and majesty. In other words, I often sold myself cheap. Far too cheaply.

Not understanding, that I was intrinsically a Woman of Worth, far more precious than rubies, I took the estimates of my worth based on the uninformed opinions of men. Men who most often, were interested in knowing me from the waist down. These men did not even notice my crown.

It took years to figure out, however, I realized it is God who made me fearfully and wonderfully. It was God's words that I would believe.

I may not have known how exquisite I was then, baby listen, I am a learned woman now. God has shown me, that I have incredible riches beyond human comprehension. He told me, for another person, I would never have to bow again.

No More AT LEAST HES

When you know you are a Queen, you won't kiss frogs. I have kissed way too many frogs in my lifetime.

Look here, a sister is not kissing another one. Not one more. I refuse to.

I found that, I have settled far too many times for the "at least he, kinds."

You know what I mean right? Discernment can be kicking you in the butt, however, low self -worth will tell your heart, "Well at least he said he loves Jesus."

Your spirit man will be saying, "Girl stay woke, he still lives with his Mama." However, desperation will try to convince you, "Well at least he got a job."

I am being transparent with you all. I have settled for some doozies. It is not because I did not get a 911, 411 and every other warning from the Holy Spirit. He was like bump the red flag, I have a burning inferno going on here. Yet, I still fell for foolishness. I guess, to be honest, I signed up for foolishness.

I did not believe, within my heart, that I could do better. I also did not have strong enough spiritual disciplines of patience, faith, and self-control to wait on God's best for my life.

I pray that you will take the time to heal, before walking, running, and diving, down the same paths I did. It can save you time, heartache, and money.

Being in denial of our issues, simply delays our breakthrough. It hurts us. It slows our progress down.

God has so many blessings He wants to release for our lives, however, He won't give them to us when He knows we will jack them up.

Growing up in the church, I knew of God.

I knew God to be my keeper. I knew I could pray to God to help me, and He would be faithful to help me.

I knew I could pray to God to heal my sick mother, and he would answer my prayers.

I was growing in my relationship with Him. I desired to please God. This desire was not stronger than my desire to please my flesh though.

At this point in my life, I loved the hand of God. I had not yet grown into a deep enough relationship to know the heart of God.

Chapter Forty-One
Just Call Me Pauline

"For what I am doing, I do not understand. For what I will to do, that I do not practice; but what I hate, that I do."- Romans 7:15

How many of you can relate to what Paul is saying here? This is the tug of war of life. When I tell you the struggle is real, I mean this thing. The blessing is, God has given us the Holy Spirit to help us win the fight.

Like, I really wanted to do right in the eyes of God. My flesh was just, so much bigger than my spirit was. Sadly, not only as a youth…

My life became a vicious cycle. I would go to church and get some, "get right" in me. I would make a celibacy vow to God. I would tell my boyfriend…ok this is the last time, because I am trying to get right with God. I cannot keep sinning like this.

Then, I would sin again. This would be followed by self-condemnation, guilt, and feeling like I fell off the wagon, and was in danger of hell's fire, so I sinned until the next Sunday. My life was a mess.

I had this constant inner turmoil of, "good girl" vs "bad girl" going on in my mind. I could not separate *what* I did from *who* I was.

God spared my life. I met some touched dudes during my bed hopping days. I mean as in, like Freddy Krueger Jr. or Little Jason.

Thank You Lord, for my life. My older relatives you to say, "God takes care of babies and fools." Listen, I was not a baby…I was surely a fool though.

I am so glad God did not give up on me, or disqualify me from the calling He had placed on my life. I can trace His hand guiding me in the direction of His calling for my life.

The omniscient, all-knowing God knew the habits, and strongholds we would have, before one of them formed.

We were still predestined to change lives for His Kingdom. Isn't this amazing and humbling.

I share these stories, not because I glory in my past. I share these stories to encourage you. God sees all and knows all. Yet, He still calls us to minister to His people. By revealing my story, I reveal the character of God. God is a Good Father. God is faithful. God is undeniably loving.

Chapter Forty-Two
I Drew Closer to God

"Draw near to God and He will draw near to you."
James 4:8

I rededicated my life to Christ when I was twenty-one years old. I was filled with the Holy Ghost. I felt so much power, joy, peace, and wholeness!

For the first time in my entire life, I felt the Presence of God! I thank God for Mother Bridges and my sister Kim, for taking me on a week day to Bethesda Temple to be baptized again.

I began reading my Bible more. I listened, more intently, to the sermons Pastor Cunningham preached. I always loved the preached Word of God. I just had not learned to apply them to my heart, or to walk them out in my life.

I was a deeply broken young woman. I did not know I was broken though.

At the age of twenty-one, I lived a torn life. I yearned to please God, yet I was angry, sad, and suffering from postpartum depression.

That mix would lead me down a road of seeking to please myself, more than I sought to please God.

I loved my son with everything in me. He was my joy. In fact, thankfully, because of him, I knew I had to get my life together.

I wanted to be a good mother and lead a life that was proper before him. In many regards, motherhood saved me from a life of sin and promiscuity.

I knew I had to take this God walk more seriously. I just did not completely know how to.

I started to sin less, however, I had not yet been made whole.

Chapter Forty-Three
God Needs You

Come out of hiding. Open up and allow God to use you. Drop the façade of perfectionism. Jesus is the Only One who is without a spot or wrinkle. I am not saying to sin or stay in a lifestyle of sin. I would never say that.

We strive to be perfect, like Jesus. I do. I love to please God. When I was younger, I wanted to please God out of fear. Now, I desire to please God because I love Him.

Snatch your masks off and bring your jacked-up selves to the alter, surrender yourself to God and be made whole.

He loves his jacked-up babies. I think I am chief in this area, yet He calls me Daughter. You know as a parent, we have to really love those special children a little extra. I am convinced, He has extra patience with me

You may find, like I have found, that you will heal as you serve Him.

The more you make yourself available to be used by God, the less time you have to focus on your pain story.

God can break us from the addiction to our pain. I can testify to this for myself. Hallelujah!

Be transparent, and lead others to the only one that can get us all the way together, God.

Chapter Forty-Four
For a Time, Such as this

God is about to do something so amazing. I know many of you just did an eye roll. You may be thinking, "Yeah, I have heard this before, but when?"

Trust God and His Perfect Timing.

He is not moving when we should.

He will move when we are ready. It is not God that is taking forever, it is His people. God is omnipresent. He is the God of yesterday, today, and forevermore.

God is not in Heaven trying to catch up to our plans. Are you kidding me? We try to play God like He is just that small. Dude, He is God!

He is not up there doubling up on his squats, bench presses, leg lifts, and arm curls, in preparation for His next move in our lives.

God is waiting on us to buff up in the spirit by studying His Word, fasting, and praying for real, not the rehearsed ones we do on Sunday mornings.

He is waiting for us to take our proper positions. We have gotten too comfortable with God. He desires intimacy with us, that is without questions. God still desires for us to have a healthy, reverential fear of Him.

When we get our emotional, physical, and spiritual selves together, we will be in a better position to carry out His good will for us

The way God is about to set His people free from the bondage of memories, of self-doubt, and past trauma, there is about to be a great rising up of God's ministers (servants) on the earth.

God is about to use, not necessarily, of a place cloaked up in titles, accolades, and prestige. God is going to use the people who are transparent enough to show you where it hurt.

After I was lied on, mistreated, accused of performing witch craft by pastors who I loved and served in the best capacity I knew how, I learned not to put my destiny in the hands of man.

It is God Who orders my steps. The reality of it is, had I known for real, WHO I was in Christ, I would not have been down for so long.

I allowed man to define me, try to box me in, then discard me when I did not fit in.

We are not victims, we are survivors. We will tell others of how God saved and delivered us out of the pits of sadness and bitterness of having been molested.

This is a process. I am aware of this. We do not go instantly, from facing the truth of what happened to us, to wanting to tell everyone about it, and how we have overcome.

In truth, recovery takes many years. Like grief, it does not happen in a linear fashion. We heal in various stages. I am not a therapist, or licensed mental health professional. I cannot offer advice on how one heals from sexual abuse.

I will encourage you to seek professional help. Sexual abuse hurts. It takes more than a scripture and prayer to get through, and this is real talk. I am a minister, so I am in no way underestimating the power of prayer. I am looking at things from a healthy, balanced perspective.

I do not want you to deal with things for as long as I did. I did not seek help for my molestation.

Being mishandled, harmed, and even dropped by those that were often in charge of us, does not stop us from receiving the rewards and benefits God has for us.

Here is the thing, nothing we have endured, or will endure will take our worthiness away.

We may feel like we lost worth after being molested. However, we did not. Our worth was given to us from God. It is intrinsic.

Another man or woman, does not have the power to take our worth, esteem, or value away from us.

I am just realizing this at the age of fifty.

Beloved, no matter who touched you, who raped you, or who made you do God awful things to them against your will, you are still precious in the eyes of your Daddy, God.

We are not tainted. We are not dirty because of what happened to us. God can take that feeling away from us and make us feel completely clean.

God did not change His mind about us. Our circumstances do not change God's thoughts towards us, nor His plans for us.

We have worth. God continues to call us beautiful, fearfully, and wonderfully made.

There is absolutely nothing we did to deserve this violation, that has left many of us scarred, broken, and bitter. NOTHING. God did not cause it, nor desire it for our lives.

Only God can heal us from this intrusion on our innocence. One way He has healed me, is by allowing me to forgive my abuser. The longer I held on to my anger, the longer he held me captive. Unforgiveness does not punish your attackers and betrayers. It instead, imprisons you.

I am here to tell you, you did not cause your sexual abuse. You can stop rehearsing the tape. As a matter of fact, rip the tape out of your mind. Destroy it right now, in the name of Jesus.

I wept for my sons and daughters, whether by blood or spirit, that have been touched inappropriately by another. I felt the pain of so many who carry this story.

The devil has held this as a noose around our necks. Beloved, we do not have to bear this weight another day.

Pray to God to heal you, and to release you from the trauma of the abuse.

It is very possible for us to be set free and enjoy life, love, and intimacy without being afraid. It is possible for us to heal from our trust issues. In fact, with God, it is possible to live as if this never happened to us.

"With men this is impossible, but with God all things are possible."- Matthew 19:26

Seek Professional help, to help you process the pain. We, as a spiritual community, undervalue the importance of psychological and psychiatric help.

There is no shame in seeking counseling and therapy. God anoints man to act as His hands, mouth, eyes, ears, arms, legs, and every extension of Himself, to bring people to a state of wholeness.

I have spent many years in counseling. There is something amazing about being able to talk to someone objective, and not having to worry about their opinions or hurting their feelings.

You need to talk about your abuse to get over it.

Burying and stuffing your emotions down, is not effective therapy-like not at all. Your issues will leak out one way or the other. It may be through sickness, and chronic unease.

It may manifest as an inability to maintain a healthy relationship. Unresolved hurt may cause you to hurt other people, who have done nothing to you, either knowingly, or unknowingly. I am a resident expert in this area.

Chapter Forty-Five
My Name is Victory

Biblically, God changed a person's name based on their destiny. He changed Abram's name which meant, father of nations, to Abraham, which meant Father of *many* nations.

God changed Sarai's name which meant, mother of nations, to Sarah, which meant mother of many nations.

You get it? They got upgrades in their names to fit the directions in which their lives were heading.

Jacob had been a or trickster, so his name fit him. When God was prepared to shift his destiny, He changed His name to Israel. This was after Jacob wrestled with the angel and won.

"Your name shall no longer be Jacob, but Israel; for you have striven with God and with men and have prevailed."- Genesis 32:28

What name from your past are you still calling yourself, that has already been changed?

Are you still calling yourself a victim, although you survived? Are you still calling yourself a divorcee, although you have blessed and single for 10 years now?

If God can get you to change your victim mentality, He can change your name. Sis, let it go.

When you change your name, you change your perspective. Change your perspective, and you will change your entire posture. I noticed, I started standing so much straighter, when I started telling my story from the angle of a survivor instead of from the angle of a victim.

While we at it, stop circling the little dot, on the doctor's forms that ask if you are, "single, divorced, married?" You all know the one I am talking about?

A sister like me is thinking, if he would not pay crap for me while we were married, what makes me think circling this here divorced option, will make him pay my medical bill now. However, I digress.

Change your name to victory. Sad story season is over! Girl, get up, straighten your crown, and live!

Look, turn your victim suit in. It is played out. Upgrade to the new suit called Victorious.

Practice telling yourself, every chance you get, that you are victorious. Walking in victory is as necessary to our lives as the very air we breathe.

We have worth. As a matter of fact, *WE ARE WORTHY!* We are the embodiment of Our Creator-God, and He is the epitome of worth. Let that sink in.

A victim mentality will keep you trapped in a victim mentality. Becoming a victim was not our choice. We became victims because someone preyed on us and took advantage of us.

Staying a victim, now that is a choice. I have been a victim of molestation, rape, and domestic violence. I am not, in any way, blowing the weight and validation off of that pain or the seriousness of those *crimes* that happened to me.

I simply cannot afford to spend the rest of my life, trapped in my victim story. God has blessed me to survive those crimes. God is a great deliverer! He did not deliver me out of physical harm, for me to be locked behind prison bars in my mind, will, and emotions.

He did not deliver you, for you to remain imprisoned either beloved. When we are stuck, WE MUST SEEK HELP!

I remember thinking that holding on to the story gave me power. Child, there is no power in that. In fact, one of the things that freed me up from being pissed off at the people that hurt me was, me sitting at home, watching life pass me by, and seeing them living their lives more abundantly.

I had to do a self -check and say, "Girl, if you do not get your entire life." I could probably find a scripture to line up with this, however, sometimes, I just have to go real sister-girl with myself (Smile). If you do not have an inner sister-girl, get one. She will bless your life.

I AM FEARFULLY AND WONDERFULLY MADE. THAT I KNOW FULLWELL. It is the *KNOWING*, or better stated, not knowing, that has been my struggle. I am determined, as I live my best life now, to have UNSHAKEABELE WORTH!

I have heard the term unshakeable faith preached repeatedly. Yet, in my quiet time, UNSHAKEABLE WORTH came into my consciousness and became a reality, that I must live for the rest of my days.

It's not just by coincidence that God would bless me with this concept. I am writing a book on knowing your worth, while still healing from shaky self-worth.

Like, there has to be more to life than rehearsing our hurts. I have done this for far too long.

Trust me, those days are OVER!

Chapter Forty-Six
It is On and Popping!

WE SHALL LIVE the great life God has available for us!

WE SHALL LIVE unapologetically full of joy and peace. I am talking the kind of peace and joy that make your enemies want to hurl.

Look, I can give zero cares about them. After what I have survived, I will not hold back my praise.

God Almighty saved my life! He changed my name!

I am no longer Mara, which means bitter. You can just call me Naomi, which means Joy! If I hear someone call me Na-Na, I won't even get mad (smile.)

Daughter, I have an amazing future designed just for you! I just need you to keep your mind on me, and I will give you peace.

I love you, I have put you through the refiner's fire, not to kill you, but to burn off the impurities that infected your line of thinking, feeling, and responding.

Now that you have obeyed me, I can saturate you with an abundant downpour of blessings."

I do not know why I had to suffer. It truly does not matter to me anymore. What matters to me now is that God gets the glory from my life.

If I have helped just one of you, there was surely purpose in my pain. God Bless you.

When we are held hostage by what happened *to* us, it prevents us from seeing what God is doing *in* us.

We never think of the beautiful things that will happen, or that even could happen.

I am not saying this accusingly. I am saying this from living a life of being trapped by my past until I started writing Beautifully Broken.

You all, that is a long time to be weighed down by the spirt of heaviness. It makes me sad to think of how long I existed, without really living.

I was in bondage. It is as if I had been given emancipation papers, but decided to hang around on the plantation.

That was not the life Jesus came to give me. He wants us to live a ridiculously, abundant life. I was living below the level of my inheritance. Listen, read what Jesus says concerning us:

"I have come that they may have life, and that they may have *it* more abundantly."-John 10:10

To this I say, this sounds mighty good to me Jesus. I do not mind if I do!

That is exactly why it is necessary for me to write! I do not want this for you. If I can help anyone, let it be you. Learn from me.

Make a decision today. Ask God to heal you of your pain and to help you break the victim mentality and cycle.

You do not have to have fancy words to pray. You do not even have to know all that you need help with.

Just simply cry out.

"God!" "Help Me!"

God hears the cry of His children. He will answer you.
"I sought the LORD, and He heard me,
And delivered me from all my fears."- Psalms 34:4

Chapter Forty-Seven
How I Made It Over

I am not sure how I would answer the question; how did you make it through such hard trials? In a word, I would have to be honest, and say, Jesus.

First and foremost, I made it because of my Great God. He never gave up on me. He would not leave me alone when I wanted to just be left alone.

God is my everything. He really is. *Everything* seems too small a word, to describe such a great and mighty God. You all, He is just so loving and kind.

He kept me through my roughest days back then, and He does the same thing now. I am so glad God is not like man. People will give you a listening ear and shoulder to lean on, for a few minutes, then dip on you.

Many people simply do not have the patience, love, and time to see you through your healing process. If you get in that $200 line and get an instantaneous healing, they have your back.

If you need them to tarry with you over some days, weeks, and Heaven forbid years, it's a wrap. I Thank God, He is not like that at all. I did not even feel His eyes roll in the spirit, when I would pray about the same issues over and over again.

God sent encouragers along the way, to remind me that God loves me. He always, carried me, when I had no strength to walk.

I sought therapy from professional therapists as often as I needed to. I even took "happy pills" as I needed to. I got over the shame of that thing.

Heck, if I could take a blood pressure pill, I could take my happy pill and keep it pushing.

I sang myself sane. I mean this literally. I sang with my church choir, and would later join the praise team at this church. Singing to God, gave me such joy. To come together, on one accord, to worship One great God, insured His presence among us.

His Presence healed me where I hurt. I learned to worship Him, whether in church or at home. I worshipped Him in the car, on my job.

While in the midst of an abusive relationship, I would literally run out the house to go to Praise Team rehearsal. It was oxygen to my cells. Singing saved me.

I learned that the more I focused on God, the less I focused on me. This was not escapism. This was learning who God was. This was the beginning of my understanding, that God is greater than me or anything that could hinder me.

I gained a new identity. I had become a worshipper. I may not have been the best alto for the twenty plus years I have sang in choirs, and on worship teams.

One thing I am certain of, I *know* God so tenderly and intimately. My worship is for real. I discovered that it was impossible to worship, and experience worry at the same time.

I fell in love with the Character of God. I fell in love with His heart, not simply His hands of blessing. My relationship with God kept me alive. It is keeping me alive today.

On my down days, I have to do the work of encouraging myself in the Lord. I have to remind myself of His track record. I sing praises unto Him.

I listen to Periscope, to a *few* solid ministers who bring a word from God that encourages my spirit.

Beloved, do you get what is going on here? I had to do something to fight for my sanity. So, do you.

God is a Healer. That is a fact. Nothing can take away from His attributes. He just is. There may be something required of you. It is wonderful that you believe God can heal you. Now put some feet to your faith.

"Thus, also faith by itself, if it does not have works, is dead."- James 2:17 NLT

I Had to Move Forward to Know My Worth

> *"Do not remember the former things,*
> *Nor consider the things of old.*
> *[19] Behold, I will do a new thing,*
> *Now it shall spring forth;*
> *Shall you not know it?"- Isaiah 43:18*

God wants us to get our *ENTIRE* lives. Like for real, aren't you tired of living broken, bitter, and bow downed? Like how long is long enough to rehearse the story?

In order to do so, I had to seek God for help to let go of my past.

If our issue is unforgiveness, we have to ask God to help us forgive. "This is easier said than done," you say. True. However, FORGIVING THE ONES THAT HURT US IS POSSIBLE.

If we say that it is impossible to forgive someone, we make Jesus out to be a liar. Jesus. Really? My Bible says anything is possible with God.

There are some hurts and betrayals that cut so deeply, it just seems like we ought to hold on to our rage. We feel like we hold power over our betrayer, as long as we are unforgiving.

Yeah, I thought so too. I *had* every right to be angry. I really did. I know there are many things going on in your present life or from your past that have you angry as well.

God is not tripping on your anger. He is tripping on what you do as a result of being angry.

"Be angry, and do not sin"- *Ephesians 4:26*

Chapter Forty-Eight
Being Set Free

"But if you do not forgive, neither will your Father in heaven forgive your trespasses."- Mark 11:26

I can remember being so hurt, devastated, and just full of rage

There is so much life for us to live! We have to make a decision to live it though. This one thing God cannot do for us. We have to decide this for ourselves.

God does not trump our free will. Do you understand this? He is all powerful, He surely could. This would make us robotic.

God wants to see us put some feet to our faith. We surely put feet to everything else. Honey listen, these feet right here kept me running, and chasing after good sex, good sales, and good food.

Why not chase the Lord down for my healing?

Why don't you? Like seriously, what do you have to lose?

Back, kicking it with God on a very frequent basis, back with Bishop Lyons, studying God's Word more, then I heard God saying, "Ask them for forgiveness."

If you all know me, I was like, "la la la la la."

Ok, I am being to "church girl" like. Let me just tell you all the truth. I did my brown girl neck roll, you know the one, when you whip your head around, real quick like? Yeah, it was more like that.

If I did not actually have the stink face going on, it was surely in my spirit. I was like hold up, what you say God?

I heard Him. I even considered God's command. I put it in the back of my mind, on my "to do list."

In all honesty, I thought it was a pretty good idea to reach out to the pastors who hurt me. I just wasn't sure I was ready to do this now. I truly had forgiven them.

I had forgiven them years ago, mostly. However, there was this residue, almost like a dark

It took a long time, however I did. I just had not considered that I needed to be forgiven. God was like, "Girl be real. Do you know who *you* are?"

That's how God talks to me. He may go all "thee and thou" with you all, we get down in modern day language (smile.)

God has crafted me into such a beautiful new creature, yet I had to get this stank off of me. The stank was the remnants of unforgiveness I carried around, for so many people that had hurt me.

I obeyed God. It was the best thing I have done. I felt immediate freedom! I reached out to leaders I loved. I did not need a response from them. I just needed them to hear my heart. God gave me reassurance that they did. It blessed my entire soul!

I don't ever want to hurt anyone. Not ever. I want to love on the people of God. I get it wrong sometimes. I have to be grown up enough to apologize. So, do you.

Listen, I have hurt people too. If you are reading this book, and I have hurt you in any way whatsoever, please forgive me. I mean this from my heart.

You have to get real with yourself, in order to be free.

I started this book blaming my father for so many of my issues. Perhaps, his issues rubbed off on me initially. However, my issues are Twila issues. My God, the man has been resting for twenty-one years.

How ridiculous does it sound for me to blame him for eating a cupcake today, or sleeping with Pooky, or blowing my check to look cute?

During this time out, the Lord has me placed in, I have had no one to blame. I had nowhere to run. I had to face my truths. I had to count the costs.

It is hard, brutal even. However, self -examination is key. Beloved, you have to acknowledge your issues in order to be delivered from them. Denial will get you nowhere.

I did. I had to admit that many of the bad men I was with was because I chose them.

We call on God to free us up. We want Him to do ALL the work, yet he requires us to do our part as well.

Part of my liberation came from facing the woman in the mirror. Listen, if you take that same energy you use trying to blame people for everything you do and feel.

Staying stuck in victim mode is like a death sentence. It really is. You might as well be on death row.

Here I am a new creature. I had just been baptized again and rededicated my heart and my gifts to God on August 28, 2017

Everything lined up.....

Brittney ministered letting go of the past during praise and worship....

Moving forward.....

I realized that I had to ask for forgiveness because, they were my spiritual parents and the bible says to honor...

Who do you need to forgive and ask forgiveness from?

Don't let the sun go down on your anger.....

Forgive them.....

Don't hold them hostage. In doing so, you are really keeping yourself captive.

Seek forgiveness.... Don't hold up their healing.

This really hurt my heart, that I had hurt someone else's heart. You know, I had been so consumed by hurt and disappointment, that it never even occurred to me that I hurt them.

Wait, if I hurt them, this gives me no room to point fingers or play the blame game. This blew the cover right off of my victim story.

It snatched the crutches away, that I had propped up with, to limp through life.

I could hear God saying, "Will thou be made whole?"

See some of us say we want to be made whole, yet we become so addicted to out victimization, that we lose sight of ever walking free and boldly again.

We have become so familiar with our limp, that we make accommodation for it. We look through warped lenses, at a dented and damaged future.

We see ourselves as a has been. When I tell you all, this thing had me bound for so long, eight years to be exact. This is why I have chosen to write eight chapters. I wrote a chapter for each of the past years I have been trapped behind unforgiveness, bitterness, fear, and depression.

My God, but today is the day of my NEW BEGINNING! I refuse to be stuck anymore. I was holding up my flight because, I did not want to forgive.

I was a beautiful butterfly trapped in a cocoon, watching those around me soar. I could not understand, for the life of me, what I was doing wrong.

I thought it was because the pastors were right. When the pastor said he doubted my ability to be able to minister to women, maybe he was right.

God was like, no baby. What I put in you is good. You will accomplish all that I created you to do.

Part of waiting on God's Best for my life, required me to take some serious self-inventory. "That is why you should examine yourself before eating the bread and drinking the cup. – 1 Corinthians 11:28."

Twila, before you preach my Word, check yourself.

Before you minister to my sheep, examine your heart and motives.

Make sure they are pure. There is a saying that has been out for years, "Don't put your mouth on me." God said, don't put your mouth on me with an impure heart.

I had no choice but to look inward.

Then, like David I cried,

Create in me a clean heart, O God,

And renew a steadfast spirit within me.

Do not cast me away from Your presence,

And do not take Your Holy Spirit from me.

Restore to me the joy of Your salvation,
And uphold me by Your generous Spirit.
Then I will teach transgressors Your ways,
And sinners shall be converted to You.
- Psalms 51:10-13

When I tell you, this Scripture got me right together, please believe me. I have heard this scripture read every first Sunday for *years,* before communion.

I read it again. The revelation God gave me today is this, "You are not even qualified to put your mouth on me (body, blood), until you do a *real heart check.*"

I had to examine myself. I can honestly say, I need a heart doctor. Thank God, I am not in ICU anymore. However, I am on that stepdown unit-Telemetry. I still need frequent heart monitoring, fruit checks, and infusions of Living Water.

Like the Woman at the well, I never want to thirst again. I do not want to thirst for the approval of man, the hand claps from the crowd, or any other temporary fix. I only long to please my Heavenly Father and to execute

His will perfectly. I desire to make Him proud and serve Him in humility.

God make me whole, so that I don't find myself again.

Much like the nurse often says roll up your sleeve, as she prepares to monitor your blood pressure, Holy Spirit, you have full access to me.

Please check my fruit and show me where I am not ripe enough, ripened and ready for servanthood, or going bad.

I want to look like You God.

I realized while I was hurt and carrying around my victim story, I had to reach back out to people I had victimized with my vicious tongue, and apologize to them.

Part of waiting on God's Best for my life required me to take some serious self-inventory. "That is why you should examine yourself before eating the bread and drinking the cup. – 1 Corinthians 11:28."

I had to examine myself

Now that I am maturing in Christ, and able to look more intently at myself, I let go of the victim mentality. I also had to take ownership of my imperfection. It is when we do this, we are able to remain humble.

It also empowers us to stop putting others on pedestals that we are unwilling to climb on.

There are no perfect people. We must exercise wisdom and discernment about who we remain in contact with. Yet, it is so freeing to finally forgive the people who took advantage of us.

Forgiveness sets us free. It gives an insurance policy, which gives us the benefit of receiving God's forgiveness when we mess up.

Forgiving people that hurt us, allows us to run forward into the blessings of God. God has so much to give us. Sometimes, we hold up our blessings by being unwilling to let go of our baggage.

I am running forward into my blessings a lot lighter now. I do not have the time, nor desire, to carry all the people from my past with me.

I am slamming those chapters closed and sealing them with the blood of Jesus. They shall not be opened again.

Don't stay trapped in yesterday. God is blessing you forward.

Chapter Forty-Nine
I Will Finish Strong

"Being Confident of this very thing, that He who begun a good work in you will complete it until the day of Jesus Christ." – Philippians 1:6

These are the most recent years of my life. They don't resemble what I thought they would. However, God has resurrected me in areas I never knew were dead. He has weaned me off the life support of other people's opinions, and taught me to think for myself.

I have confronted the gut wrenching pain of having been both molested and abused. I had hidden this hurt so deep inside of me. Snatching the scab off my partially healed scars, was very difficult.

As a nurse, I learned that some wounds heal best when open to air.

My God, please catch this. Keeping your secret buried in a dark place, may arrest you healing and cause you to develop treatment resistant infections.

Get to a safe place, and get some help with your issues. Daughter, you have hemorrhaged too long. You will be in a better place to love and receive love again, once you receive help with your issues of pain, fear, mistrust, and unforgiveness.

God specializes in our issues. The Woman with the Issue Blood is my hero. She had been ostracized because of her hemorrhaging. Abandonment by her friends could not kill her press.

Failed attempts at healing did not dissuade her from exercising her faith to try, one more time, to be healed.

She gave herself the most awesome pep talk in history, AND stretched her faith for her healing.

"For she said within herself, If I may but touch his garment, I shall be whole." -Matthew 9:21 KJV

She pressed through the crowd of her pain, frustration, financial barriers, and past treatment history.

See, she was desperate enough to be healed, that she did not mind crawling to get it. How badly do you want yours?

Your brokenness does not have to be the end of you.

It could simply be, an indication that you need to try something new. Where is your faith? Do you have hem reaching faith?

Her deliverance began with what she said within herself. Like her, I continue to press my way to the hem of Jesus' to be made WHOLE.

Healing is good. I have spent most of my sick times, praying to be healed. I didn't realize, I could also be made whole. I stopped my press too early in the game.

Wholeness, is a much deeper level of wellness, in which there is nothing missing, and nothing broken,

Won't you be made whole?

Press forward. Now that you know that your past has no power. Reach out. Stretch your faith. Get the help you need to live a life more abundantly, like Christ desires for you.

Beloved, I am in the press as well. I am not satisfied with temporary healing. I appreciate the good days I have here and there. I do however, keep reaching for Jesus and going to believe God for my complete wholeness

I am bringing you all along with me. Then we can encourage others to come see a Man... like the Woman at the Well did.

Chapter Fifty
My Heart Still Beats

Before I leaned into writing this book, I felt so discontent. I knew God had given me so many stories to tell. However, I struggled with so much sadness.

I went through a season of migraine headaches, for one year straight. This was recent, you all. I am not talking way back then, I am talking 2015-2017. Well, make that almost, two years straight.

I would become so disheartened. I wondered why God placed so much inside of me, without the physical stamina and strength to complete His will. I felt trapped inside of my own body.

Then, one morning it happened. As I lay in bed trying to convince myself to go back to sleep, I heard the most beautiful thing...my heartbeat. I quieted myself to listen to its rhythm. Then, it hit me. I am ALIVE! Tears flowed down my cheek as I really realized, that I SURVIVED!

It's one thing to know this with my intellect. However, to really catch this thing in my spirit?! My God! I inclined my ear to my cadence of my heart, that beat ever so strongly and realized, that though it has been broken, bruised, and abandoned, my heart never lost its rhythm.

Nothing internal, nor external could destroy the electrophysiology of my heartbeat. Nothing from my past or present flatlined, its call.

No trial or tribulation could abort its destiny or convince it to give up the fight-NO THING.

My heart pumps oxygenated blood, to every cell in my body to keep me alive.......STILL.

Check your pulse! Your heart is still beating too. Baby listen, as long as we have a heartbeat, we have another opportunity to experience God's goodness on this side of Heaven.

I believe I will run on and see what the end will bring. There are some good things that I am believing God for. For once in my life, I believe I am worth them all! Bring the blessings on God!

When I do make it to Heaven, I want all of the presents, blessings, and gifts that I was supposed to be enjoying on earth, to be SPENT UP! I will not be passing through this way again. So, while I have a chance, TURN DOWN FOR WHAT?!

Chapter Fifty-One
We Have to Be Savage!

I Once Was Blind

God opened my eyes. I was so excited about writing a book to help heal His people of the wounds of their pasts. However, you know it had to hit me first.

God revealed the blind spots in my mind, heart, and spirit. God healed this little girl, and told her to Arise! God allowed me to see the areas of my heart that had not healed properly.

God blessed me to become vulnerable. There is no shame in vulnerability. There is healing in being real before God.

God revealed to me that I had some places where I was still broken, bitter, and living as if I were still being battered. I had to be exposed. Laying out on the examination table was so uncomfortable. Oh, my goodness.

You know how at the doctor's office, they give you that really thin, good-for-nothing-paper towel-of-a sheet to cover up with? Yes, that was me, trying to cover up my ginormous issues before an ALL-SEEING GOD.

I felt like I was stretched out before Cyclops and His piercing glaze was on the parts of my heart I tried to coverup. Needless to say, writing, brought out the good, the bad, and the ugly parts of me. I thank God for this process though. I would have never known, there were parts of me that still needed a healing, had I not gone through this process of stripping down.

I had to lay out my unforgiveness for myself, my attackers, my abusers, and everyone I believed wronged me. I had to give up my righteous indignation and allow God to carry this for me. After all, after a while, this festers into bitterness and rage.

I had to lay all of this stuff at the feet of Jesus. I had to lay aside these weights. You see, there are big sins that I prided myself in not committing any more. In actuality, there is never room for pride, because if I am ever dependent on God's grace and mercy to keep me from slipping.

Yet, there are those sins that we are less cognizant of, that infect our ministry. God is like okay, you are no longer committing adultery, but how is your heart?

You don't drink anymore, but who are you holding a grudge against?

See God wants us completely free. Truthfully, I was living partially free to say it mildly.

I am now perpetually learning and KNOWING MY WORTH! I AM ALL OF THAT AND A BAG OF CHIPS, DIP, SWEET TEA, AND THEN SOME!

NOT ON MY OWN, BUT IN CHRIST. I no longer owe anyone explanations for who I am. I just am who I am. Do you know who my Daddy is? He is, the Great I Am.

I AM FEARFULLY AND WONDERFULLY MADE. THAT I KNOW FULLWELL. It is the *KNOWING*, or better stated, not knowing that has been my struggle. I am determined as I live my best life now, to have UNSHAKEABELE WORTH!

I have heard the term unshakeable faith preached over and over again. Yet, in my quiet time, UNSHAKEABLE WORTH came into my consciousness and became a reality that I must live for the rest of my days.

It's not just by coincidence that God would bless me with this concept. I am writing a book on knowing your worth, while still healing from shaky self -worth. I am working a job where I feel I am not valued, and I am confident that I am one of the most well-rounded nurses there.

Then it occurred to me, with unshakeable worth, although hurt and attacks come, it doesn't destroy your inner sanctum and value.

I am praying that God blesses us all with unshakeable worth.

I am learning to embrace all of the qualities of myself.

I appreciate how I think, how I love, how I create, how I have survived. I appreciate myself If I do nothing but chill.

I appreciate the inner qualities about myself, that no one knows. I love me. I love spending time alone. I love the thoughts I think. I no longer need to bounce them off of someone else, and for them to tell me they are good thoughts. The thoughts are good because I said they are.

I pray for you to reach this place of self -appreciation in your life also. The peace that comes alone with it is irreplaceable. I know what it is to spend your life and waste your time chasing the approval of man.

As long as you place that much power in the hands of another human, you give them the power to make or break you. It is like handing the strings of your peace over to a puppeteer. However, they decide to yank your strings in the moment, is the direction in which your thoughts, will, and emotions will follow.

The only being that should EVER have that much control over us, is God. The only human that should be in control of our emotions, is us.

Chapter Fifty-Two
We Have Been Made New

"Therefore, if anyone is in Christ, he is a new creature; the old things passed away; behold, new things have come." – 2 Corinthians 5:17 (NASB)

I have no obligation to carry on with my past habits, and mindsets. For what? They did not work for me then. I am so phenomenally made, I can switch it up at any time. So can you!

Now walk it out!

Don't you dare settle for living in the box of your past. You are out of the box now. You can't be boxed in. The possibilities for your life are immeasurable. They are endless! You do know Who holds the key right?

Like for real, do you know Who has predestined your amazing future? I am excited for us!

"For those whom He foreknew, He also predestined to become conformed to the image of His Son," -Romans 8:29 NASB

Just simply say, "God help me." Some of my most effect prayers have been, "God help me!" or "Jesus!" I did not have the time, nor energy to try to remember a spooky, deep, or complicated prayer formula. God does not need all of that. He is GOD. He knows what we need before we ever ask.

He specializes in people with issues. Have you read anything I have written? I was, and am, a woman with issues, yet God still loves me, calls me, uses me, and favors me. God showers me with unmerited favor.

Man, I love God. The more He loves me, the more I love and appreciate Him.

My God! You ever just have the Holy Spirit just highjack the keyboard?

Baby, the breakthrough is in the reach! You have to believe you are healed, before you see the manifestation. All we are required to do is reach for it! The reach may be hard, the walk to Jesus, may be difficult, however the reward is definitely worth it.

What is more difficult than what you have already endured? Like the Woman with the Issue of Blood, I have already bled everywhere. I have already lost my loved ones. I've already been ostracized and edged out of my community.

People already look at me strange. They already turn their noses up at me. So what?! I believe God! If I got to crawl to my Redeemer, that's what I will do. I know each inch I make forward, I am closer to my breakthrough.

My question to you today is, *how bad do you want it?*

I decided I was going to be savage like this woman. I will stop at nothing to be whole. I am worth it, and God is able. With this combination, it shall come to pass.

The next time somebody tells you, you act like a girl, or cry like a woman, tell them "Thank you."

This Woman is a Beast! Arise!

I have come such a long way through this writing process. I pray that you have grown as well. It is my heart's desire to have you grow forward and realize that you are not alone.

God has been with you, and he will never leave you. It is possible for you to have joy everlasting. Peace, which passes all understanding, shall be ours.

Beauty for ashes, is Jesus' promise to us. We must give Him our ashes, those things that are dead, negative, and weigh us down, in order to receive His supernatural and unfading love.

In other words, hand God your sad, heavy, victim, story, and receive the beauty, liberty, and breath of fresh air of being a victor. Child of God, victory looks good on you.

WAIT…

On October 24, 2017, I was in my prayer closet wondering why I could not push send to my editor. I had worked tirelessly on this book for six to eight hours each day, on top of working eight to ten hours daily for my job.

I prayed, cried, and stayed on my face before God, to pour through me for His people. I am confident that He did just that. God is faithful. Then, God spoke to me.

My prayer closed is my shower you all. I almost did a matrix flip out of that bad boy. The Revelation He gave me is AMAZING. God told me, "Yes, Daughter. You have done well to help My people. Now let me make you well, and make you free."

Chapter Fifty-Three
Daughter

As abruptly as I typed that "wait," above, is just how the Holy Spirit arrested me. I just love Him. He will grab our attention anyway He needs to.

It was painful to undress before you all, and tell you all about events that had happened to me when I was nine years old and seventeen years old. However, those events were farther removed from me than the latest time I felt stripped and discarded.

The Holy Spirit has been prompting me to open up and share this story. I have tried to ignore His voice. I have spent ten chapters telling you to "undress", "show God where it hurts", "be real," and "crawl if you have to." I meant every word of it. Every word, I have shared has been my truth.

Every Scripture is truth, of course. I realized in my prayer closet, and even as I type, that although I thought I was naked before God, I still had on my underclothes.

God help me to uncover this last pain completely Lord, so I can be made WHOLE!!!!!!

Chapter Fifty-Four
A Life Surrendered

"Therefore, I urge you, brethren, by the mercies of God, to present your bodies a living and holy sacrifice, acceptable to God, which is your spiritual service of worship. And do not be conformed to this world, but be transformed by the renewing of your mind, so that you may prove what the will of God is, that which is good acceptable and perfect." -Romans 12:1-2 NASB

Reverend George Hawkins, whom I affectionately called Papi, became my first spiritual father. He was the kindest, yet most steadfast men I knew. He taught me this scripture, and demanded I live it.

I promise, Papi could do a fruit check on me on the spot. He would ask, "How are you doing daughter?" I would spill my guts and ask for prayer. I laugh as I type this. He loved me, so unconditionally. I love and miss you Papi. Rest in Heavenly peace.

He helped me want to please God with my entire life. Papi saw my worth! He saw my treasure. I would begin to see my treasure as well. I would start to hold my head just a little bit higher because, He called me daughter.

Finally, I was someone's daughter.

By the time I was licensed to preach, I thought God had delivered me from every need to be approved by man.

Still not perceiving that my worth came from within me, I chased it in the applause of my pastor. My father was no longer alive to tell me, "good job," so I looked around in the crowd for applause.

The problem with approval from the crowd is, the crowd becomes your demigod. Only depend on God for approval. He is the one Who created you in His image. He made you fearfully and wonderfully. Wonderful are *His* works.

I aimed to please God. I would preach to heal the broken, lead the lost to Christ, *and* hope to make my pastors proud. They were such phenomenal preachers. I truly wanted to be like them.

God could have descended on me like a Dove, and said, "This is my Daughter in Whom I am well pleased." I would have said, "Aww thank you God, but are they pleased too?"

My perspective was messed up. My approval addiction was at an all-time high.

It was necessary for God to snatch me up out of there and place me in a time out. He had to teach me to love myself. God had to teach me to value myself. God had to teach me my *worth.*

I breathed worth into so many women, during the eighteen months that I led them, that I did not put the oxygen mask on myself. This has been my time to breathe so that I could live.

In true Twila fashion, I cared so much for others, that I neglected myself. I held the bandage to stop others from bleeding, and failed to see that I was bleeding out. I was losing vitality, quickly. God called a time out.

He knew I would never leave the women I adored, willingly. He worked the devastation of my being asked to step down from leading, for the good.

"And we know [with great confidence] that God [who is deeply concerned about us] causes all things to work together [as a plan] for good for those who love God, to those who are called according to His plan and purpose."
– Romans 8:28 AMP

I knew without a doubt that God loved me. I heard clearly from Him. My relationship was solid with the Lord. We hung out daily.

I am not saying I was anywhere near perfect, what I am saying is, I knew His voice. I may not have always heeded to it, but I knew it. When I accepted my calling, and began to walk in ministry, I was married and raising four children.

The Lord had brought me through the devastation of losing both of my parents, several years prior, and enduring some things, I could not quite explain, at home now.

I knew Him to be my keeper. I knew the Lord to be my comforter. I had encountered God as Daddy, I had bumped up against God as my King. I had become a worshipper. Even still, I wanted my pastor's approval. I wanted to make him proud, much like a child wants to please their parent.

As I preached my Licensing Sermon, I could feel the Holy Spirit all over me. I knew my Heavenly Father was smiling upon me. I looked over and saw my Pastor smiling. I knew that he was pleased. I thought. "Yes!"

I hope you all are hearing this in the spirit, as the Lord is giving this to me. I was still walking around, seeking approval. I *still* sought the approval of man, although it was God Himself, that put the fire in my belly to preach and teach His word.

The only One I aim to please, is God *today*. God had to take me through a process to heal however. Healing for me did not come easy either.

Chapter Fifty-Five
Women's Ministry

"Study and do your best to present yourself to God approved, a workman [tested by trial] who has no reason to be ashamed, accurately handling and skillfully teaching the word of truth." -2 Timothy 2:15

I would become a cutting-edge leader of the women's ministry at this church. Oh my Goodness! The ideas, creativity, and anointing *God* poured through me, was simply mind blowing. God stirred up gifts in me, that I could have never imagined existed. I volunteered them all to this church.

I did not lead haphazardly. I stayed on my face before God, studied His Word, prayed, fasted, went to Seminary to grow in my understanding of Women in Theology.

.

There was such a powerful anointing on my life, that people began to come to the Sunday School class that I taught because, they heard "So and So" had been healed.

Listen, I was always 100% clear with people. I am nobody. All things are possible, only through Christ.

I was never confused about whose power was healing them. I always told them to praise God. I was merely a willing conduit of His work. He could flow through me how He chose.

I Was Still That Little Girl

I stood flatfooted and preached with Holy Ghost POWER!

Once asked to step down, I lost EVERY OUNCE OF CONFIDENCE I ever had as a preacher. EVERY OUNCE. This is what happens when you put too much weight in what men say, and not what God says about you.

I know the preacher is still inside of me. I trust God to fan the flame and make her roar again. I am being painfully honest with you. I want you all to learn from my mistakes, so you don't hurt like I hurt.

When my former pastor told me, there was no room in His church for *my kind of gifts,* I again felt rejected, mishandled, and molested by someone, whose love and approval I desired.

God has taught me, throughout this writing process, that this entire book was not only to heal the women from without, that will read this story and relate.

God says, this woman is very much for the woman that is within, that has been bowed over in pain for so many years, and could not straighten her way up. He says to me today, Arise Twila. You Have Worth and You are Healed from Your Infirmities.

Arise Woman of Worth! Arise

1.	Serve God and Him only.

2.	Seek Validation from God and Him Only.

3.	If you are dealing with a people pleasing spirit, pray for deliverance and seek Spiritual Counseling from *trustworthy* leaders.

4.	Seek Counseling.

5.	Had I known my worth, the effects of another man and woman's words, would not have been so devastating.

6.	Never ever, take stock in the hype of the crowd. Jesus learned this. On Palm Sunday, the Crowed praised Him and Sang, "Hosanna." Just a few days later, they yelled with hatred and contempt, "Crucify Him, Crucify Him!"

7.	I have to, *encourage myself* in the Lord.

8.	God showed me that it is unfair to put pastors or any other leader upon a pedestal. They are no more perfect than I am.

9.   God showed me how to forgive them, and to ask them for forgiveness.

10.   God taught me not seek my worth from other people. They cannot give me, what He has already deposited into me.

Take time and write down anything that stuck out to you from this last story. Have you been walking around hurting and bitter from church hurt?

Have you been holding others to a standard you would not be able to keep?

Pray to God and ask for forgiveness. Believe in Him for a clean slate.

Also, ask God to show you who you need to make amends with, and set a plan in place to make things right.

_____

_____

_____

_____

_____

_____

_____

_____

_____

_____

_____

_____

Most often the thing blocking us from walking freely in our amazing destiny, is a spirit polluted with unforgiveness. That stuff ways us down. It is time to lose some weight. Queens, we are too royal to be carrying around all this extra baggage.

Start forgiving today. Please do not let unforgiveness, cloud your vision for as long as I did. I really thought I had forgiven my parents, friends, *myself,* pastors, you name it, only to find out there was still residue hanging around and keeping me from living my best life right now.

Listen, I am trying to live every bit of by Queendom out to the max. I simply do not have time to drag old stuff with me. That stuff is dead.

I'll be darned, if the people that hurt me have more fun in my life, than me. Hey, call this mentality whatever, I mean this thing. I have lived this martyr existence and it has gotten me nowhere but sick, busted, and disgusted.

Chapter Fifty-Six
Queen Behavior Begins in the Mind

"For as he thinketh in his heart, so is he,"-Proverbs 23:7

We must see ourselves as queens, before we ever *feel* like a queen. The way we see ourselves, self-perspective, or our view of self, has everything to do with how we treat ourselves, how we carry ourselves, whether or not we set proper boundaries, and how we allow others to treat us.

I will be honest, I am just growing into my queendom. I am okay with this though. I cannot waste time grieving all the time, I allowed this person to hurt me, or that person to hurt me. I have done that for long enough. I have too much living to do, know that I realize my worth.

We deserve Kings. Nothing Less.

If we are going to marry kings, we are going to have to stop dating frogs.

God please heal our perspectives of self. Bless us to see ourselves through Your eyes. In the name of Jesus, I pray, Amen.

Fast and pray. Pray intentional prayers. If you struggle with self -confidence. Ask God to give you self-confidence. It is not deep. Now, be prepared.

God is not like a Fairy, granting wishes. If you are asking Him for confidence, He will likely put you in a situation, to build your situation.

Listen, we all have a story. Not knowing our worth, is NO EXCUSE for not learning our worth. Okay, we did not know our worth before, got it. Get with some positive sisters or brothers to speak life into you, and that will hold you accountable for your janky behavior.

Now that you are walking in worthiness.

You will have to reexamine some of your patterns. You will have to realize, some of the frogs you dated were just because you were horny or lonely-yeah, I do not have a scripture for this one.

Get your life. Do better. The better we believe about ourselves, the better we will attract to ourselves. I am like 1000% Christian. I started seeing people posting all the stuff about energy on Facebook. Baby Listen, when I started attracting men from a whole new level in life, I had to give God a High Praise.

I felt like my girl...I done had to fight, dang near all my life.

Before this, I would be like dang, God, let me get back on this alter. Now, I know He is changing the inside of me.

Quit dating losers. Did the preacher say that? YES!

Love everybody. Pray for everybody. There is not one scripture that says, date everybody. No, not one.

See yourself as the QUEEN you are and believe God is getting your KING together.

Truthfully, it has been within the last year, that I have learned to walk in my Queendom alone. God had to show me my worth was not connected to a friendship, position, or connection, other than, the one I have with Him.

Chapter Fifty-Seven
Better is Coming!

God's has more for you! He has more for me! Doesn't that excite you? I do not know about you, but after all the hell that I have been through, I am ready for BETTER!

BETTER

My God! I am so excited about this chapter in my life! I know what it is to be broken; broken-hearted, broken spirted, just broken. I know what it is to feel betrayed.

In this season, God has made me better. He had to crush me, so the oil could pour forth. He told me that He is breaking me beautifully. He has hidden me in His Secret Place, not because I was inadequate, he was perfecting me. He was making me BETTER.

EVERYTHING He is doing in my life, is setting me up for the best days of my life. My suffering days are over. My crying days are over. My *need* for applause, smiles, titles, and a chance to stand behind another man's pulpit are over.

I know who I am. I AM FEARFULLY AND
WONDERFULLY MADE, MARVELOUS ARE GOD'S
WORKS, AND I AM ONE OF HIS WORKS. YOU CAN
JUST CALL ME, "LADY MARVELOUS."

*"But now He has obtained a more excellent ministry,
by as much as He is also the mediator of a better
covenant, which has been enacted on better promises."-
Hebrews 8:6*

Better is Here for all of us! Better is Here through
Jesus Christ!

Decree these things, over your life every day! *God, I
thank You for: BETTER service to You, BETTER worship
to you, BETTER praise to You, I Praise you God for a
BETTER relationship with You, I thank you for BETTER
obedience, and submission to YOU LORD.*

*I thank YOU GOD, for BETTER time spent in quiet
time with YOU LORD. I Thank YOU, FOR BETTER SELF
-WORTH. I thank YOU, FOR BETTER SELF- LOVE. I
thank you God, for BETTER SELF-RESPECT. I thank
you GOD for making my thirsty soul, BETTER!*

I thank you, for saving my sons and making them BETTER! I thank you, for making my daughters and my grandchildren, BETTER! I thank you, God for making my spending habits, BETTER! I thank you, for healing every abused man and woman reading these words, BETTER!

Thank you, God for making every saddened heart, and mind, BETTER! God thank You, for the JESUS that makes all things, BETTER!!!

God, I thank you for BETTER peace, BETTER joy, BETTER love, BETTER faith, BETTER rest, BETTER hope, BETTER health, BETTER wealth, BETTER self-control, BETTER vision, BETTER.

GOD, WE THANK AND PRAISE YOU FOR BETTER!!!!!!!

I AM A WOMAN OF WORTH.
I AM ROYALTY

ARISE WOMAN OF WORTH, ARISE!

"An excellent woman [one who is spiritual, capable, intelligent, and virtuous], who is he who can find her?

Her value is more precious than jewels and her worth is far above rubies or pearls."- Proverbs 31:10 AMP

Conclusion

Though I was molested as small and innocent girl, bruised, yet I thrived. Licensed, applauded, then accused, and yet I rise.

God has kept me alive! I may still cry and ask Him "why?" Why God, would you show me my true passion in life, then allow it to be ripped from my arms like a baby still nursing from my breast?

For many years, eight to be exact, I listened, but heard no reply. Now, as I conclude this book, God allows me to see, the baby I had to let go of, was simply the beginning, and not the end of me.

You see, my view of my worth was attached to a person, position, or title, it seems. While my Heavenly Father was determined to teach me, that the wealth, anointing, and beauty abides **WITHIN ME.**

I hear the Holy Spirit saying, I had not lost my first baby-the women's ministry, this baby, my first book would have never been birthed.

The blessing in my story is, that the women I used to lead are still living, growing, striving, preaching, teaching, and doing great things for the Kingdom of God!

My rainbow baby, the baby of promise after the loss of a baby, would never have been birthed. Had the pastor not grabbed my hand and told me, "I never thought you could lead the Women's Ministry in the first place."

ARISE WOMAN OF WORTH, is my Baby of Promise!

Baby, you have to know that you know, your worth! You have to have unshakeable worth!

God showed me that my self-worth was shaky, or else the words of my leader would never have taken me out like that. I would have cried, and even felt devastation. However, I would never have felt suicidal. *Take my life?*

My God.

If you have self-worth issues, listen to me, RUN and get professional help! I never in life, want anyone to suffer like I did. I have faith that you can see how dangerous this can be. There is no room for pride here, do you hear me?

I do not care if you are the pastor of the church. I do not care if you are the archbishop. Your life, and the lives

of those around you, depend on you getting the help you
need.

God desires for us to live in peace, love, and joy. He
does not want His children to be miserable. I had to go to
counseling after these events in my life. I fell into the
deepest of depression. I had no clue that I still had worth.
This is what happens when you define your equity based
on what you do, instead of who you are. *Beloved you
have worth.*

Power belongs to God, and God dwells within us in the
person of His Holy Spirit. *You are a force to be reckoned
with.* They cannot fool with you. Recognize, that when
people talk about you and start trying to tear you down,
they already see how big you are.

Please, please, please, examine yourselves and ask
God to give you a proper assignment of power, and a
healthy self-worth.

All along, I thought I was writing to tell you all to Arise
and snatch back your power and worth. All along, God

was telling me to do the same thing too. I am so in awe of God!

Arise Sisters! We Have Worth! Straighten your Crowns, we are Taking Over! We refuse to settle for less than God's best for our lives. We do not have to.

No More "AT LEAST HES"

Women of Worth, we do not have to settle ever again.

I dated more at-least-he's. At least he's got a job. Yeah well, he is paying Child Support on 8 kids, so you have to fit the bill EVERY TIME.

Well, at least he said he love me. Yeah, after he cheated for the what, tenth time? Well... at least he bought my baby some Jordan's. Girl please, He made an investment. He is not paying rent, mortgage, life insurance, gas, electric, cable, or buying groceries.

Women of Worth we must Arise. We are Queens.

I did not know my worth, however, I know my worth now, and I will dine alone, before I waste my time with another AT LEAST HES.

We must do the work of self-examination, healing, and growth before we are in position to receive our next level blessings.

Wait on the Lord, Women of Worth. Our blessings are on the way!

"Wait on the Lord;

Be of good courage,

And He shall strengthen your heart;

Wait, I say, on the Lord!" – Psalms 27: 14

Do not give up on your life because God allowed something to be taken from you, whether in the natural, or in the spirit. God will always replace what you lost with a *rainbow baby.* God has something He wants to birth through you!

He wants to give you Beauty for Ashes!

"The Spirit of the Lord GOD is upon me; because the LORD hath anointed me to preach good tidings unto the meek; he hath sent me to bind up the brokenhearted, to proclaim liberty to the captives, and the opening of the prison to them that are bound;

To proclaim the acceptable year of the LORD, and the day of vengeance of our God; to comfort all that mourn;

To appoint unto them that mourn in Zion, to give unto them beauty for ashes, the oil of joy for mourning, the garment of praise for the spirit of heaviness; that they might be called trees of righteousness, the planting of the LORD, that he might be glorified." – Isaiah 61:1-3 KJV

About the Author

Twila R. Favors is a preacher, teacher, keynote conference speaker, and lover of God's people. She desires more than anything, to see ALL of God's people made WHOLE.

Twila loves hanging out with her friends and family. She spends every second she gets, loving on the joy of her life, her granddaughter Kayla.

For Booking information, email Twila at authortwilafavors.com. You can follow her on Facebook at Author Twila R. Favors.

RESOURCES

Resources Available 24 Hours a Day

National Sexual Assault Hotline- 1-800-656-4673
They offer assistance to anyone dealing with issues surrounding molestation, rape, sexual assault, and domestic violence.

National Domestic Violence Hotline -1-800-799-SAFE (7233). Advocates are available 24/7. Anonymous and confidential.
National Domestic Violence Hotline also offers:
Loveisrespect.org – A confidential website for Domestic Violence Survivors
Text Services – Simply text **Loveis** (22522) This will get you connected with an advocate. -Everything remains confidential.

National Suicide Prevention Hotline- 1-800-273-TALK (8255) Advocates are available around the clock to speak with you.

Text Crisis Line

741741-Texting this number will connect you with a Counselor that you can talk through your feelings with. They are available 24 hours a day.

Bible References

All Scripture References are from the New King James Version Bible unless otherwise stated.

Amplified Bible (Amplified)

New King James Bible (NKJV)
King James Version (KJV)
The Message Bible (MSG)
New American Standard Bible (NASB)
New Revised Standard Bible (NRSV)

New Living Translation Bible (NLT)

Merriam Webster Dictionary

www.ingramcontent.com/pod-product-compliance
Lightning Source LLC
Chambersburg PA
CBHW021924040426
42448CB00008B/893